PRAISE FOR *LEAD YOUR TEAM TO WIN*

"In *Lead Your Team to Win*, Maxine Attong suggests that every managerial style include practices used by contemporary executives and life coaches such as the creation of collaborative 'safe spaces,' where employees can take risks and develop their thoughts. Maxine then shares her experiences with using a similar approach for motivating employees when she becomes vice president of a firm. The result is success for all: herself, her employees, and the organization."

—Patrick Buckley, CPA, CMA, PhD, Ottawa, Canada

"*Lead Your Team To Win* is an intriguing book that is very timely in highlighting the need to have a 'safe space' in the workplace. Employees are overwhelmed today with so much going on in their lives and not being able to cope with the stress of managing so many things. Often technology is a block in simplifying thoughts as one is continuously bombarded with data, information, emails, phone calls, and other distractions vying for our attention. Derailing is often the result. This is when the leader steps in and helps the team members to recover quickly by offering them the 'safe space'—a place where individuals and teams can be themselves, show their vulnerability, and, above all, trust and support each other. How leaders can implement this is what this book is all about."

—Sunita Sinha, VP of organizational effectiveness at a forty-billion dollar diversified conglomerate headquartered in India

"*Lead Your Team to Win* is a practical book filled with insights, stories, and experiences that will help any manager. The workplace is becoming more complex and difficult to navigate. Employees are expecting more, while companies need to do more with less. This creates immense strain for managers. *Lead Your Team to Win* provides wonderful methods to make this challenge more rewarding and productive."

—Greg Zlevor, President of Westwood International, Founder of The Leadership Project and FOG

"All of us who have worked in corporate environments will have experienced the kind of scenarios that Maxine Attong captures in her new book. Many of us will also have experienced managers and leaders at their best and at their worst when it comes to handling situations and motivating teams. While I for one can think of some great bosses who have applied many of the approaches advocated here, there are plenty for whom this would be a great dose of insight and application. The 'safe space' concept as expressed here was new to me; it doesn't just refer to a physical space—rather an approach. This is certainly easier to read about than to implement—especially since many workplace cultures do not have the scale nor the ability to separate work operations and work innovation. This is especially true in our current diverse workforce where, for some, work is a means to an end, and, for others, work is a place for full expression of abilities and talent. But that's not to say we shouldn't try. This book provides great tools to help leaders focus on assisting people in getting the most out of their work—and their work more out of them."

—Mohan Yogendran, Director, Rockpools (internal executive recruitment firm), United Kingdom

"Maxine Attong's *Lead Your Team To Win* is a refreshing and important exploration of what it means to be a leader. It's been fashionable for business books to include 'authenticity' in their lists of essential leadership qualities, but few have defined what 'being authentic' really means. Maxine goes straight to the heart of it. Her insight is as powerful as it is simple: there's no difference between the professional you and the personal you. The way to be authentic is to consciously bring your self to the office—every day. That may be easier to say than to achieve, but Maxine demonstrates that those who do so can lead better, be better, and, perhaps most importantly, show their colleagues the way to bring their genuine selves to the workplace as well. *Lead Your Team To Win* is one of those rare books that leaves you saying, 'Well, of course that's true. It's so obvious.' Obvious perhaps, but very much in need of saying—and hearing."

—Tim Hurson, author of *Think Better and Never Be Closing*

"While reading this, I noticed a calming effect come over me. I love the genuine definition of what it means to create a 'safe space.' What a highly conscious concept that requires someone to truly come from a deep sense of a 'we all win or we don't play' mindset. When we hear the concept of creating a 'safe space,' we think social work and psychology. However, to bring this concept into business and corporate environments is innovative and respects the human condition. Keeping things private and having a 'stiff upper lip' is old school and creates pressure. The ability to have the skills to develop this behavior without judgment while keeping confidences is a high vision to hold. This book will challenge leaders to look within and calm their egos."

—Connie Kadansky, PCC, sales call reluctance coach and trainer

"*Lead Your Team To Win* suggests that there is no real separation between our personal and professional lives since one ultimately affects the other. The leader's job is to help the team members to keep this in balance and to assist the members to park feelings and get the job done."

—Libby Anderson, M.S. SPHR, TalentForce Solutions

"Leaders have struggled for years with the *how* of motivating their teams to stay engaged. In *Lead Your Team to Win*, Maxine gently uses empathy and listening as powerful tools to build and maintain productivity. The work will always get done by someone, but the how is what makes us come back and give our all. It is refreshing to read that going back to the human touch will bring our teams and employees together."

—Patricia Weiland, M.A., PCC

"Maxine Attong's latest book reveals her approach to leading teams to success. An accomplished manager, Maxine had experienced first-hand the frustrations of feeling solely responsible for the team's success. She grew to realize that there were other ways of leading teams. Bringing lessons from the fields of facilitation and coaching, Maxine embarked on an approach to leadership that built and empowered team members to collaborate on the path to delivering great results. In this book, Maxine tells the story of how she brought her convictions into the workplace, transforming the team's experience and leading them to personal and professional success. There are lessons here for all of us who lead teams."

—Michael Randel, management consultant and facilitator, Global 100 Thought Leader in Trustworthy Business

"*Lead Your Team to Win* brings a totally new dimension to leadership. It offers a perspective on how to strike balance between personal and professional lives so as to bring out the full potential of team members. Maxine Attong brings a practical life experience to bear on the concept of leadership. Organizational leadership needs to evolve to meet the daily demands of team members and create an environment in which they take pride in collaborating in a joint effort with their leader for the common good of the organization. The most important qualities that leaders need to demonstrate are trust and honesty in order to provide a 'safe space' so that team members can perform to the best of their abilities. *Lead Your Team to Win* thus has the potential of taking one's leadership abilities to a new height, and in today's dynamic economy and work reality, it will be a useful guide in creating a winning team."

—Thomas Asare, MSc, FCCA, CFE, CFC, MCMI, director of programming, budgeting, finance, and accounting, African Union

ACHIEVE OPTIMAL PERFORMANCE
BY PROVIDING **A SAFE SPACE** FOR EMPLOYEES

Lead Your Team to Win

Maxine Attong

RIVER GROVE
BOOKS

Published by River Grove Books
Austin, TX
www.rivergrovebooks.com

Distributed by River Grove Books

For ordering information or special discounts for bulk purchases, please contact River Grove Books at PO Box 91869, Austin, TX 78709, 512.891.6100.

Design and composition by Greenleaf Book Group
Cover design by Greenleaf Book Group

Cataloging-in-Publication data
Attong, Maxine.
  Lead your team to win : achieve optimal performance by providing a safe space for employees / Maxine Attong.—First edition.
    pages ; cm
  Issued also as an ebook.

  1. Attong, Maxine. 2. Employees—Counseling of. 3. Personnel management.
4. Teams in the workplace. 5. Leadership. I. Title.

HF5549.5.C8 A88 2014
658.385   2014945272

Print ISBN: 978-1-63299-009-9
eBook ISBN: 978-1-63299-010-5
First Edition

For my niece Selena Ferrier Langton.
I am your safe space.

Acknowledgments

Throughout my professional career, I've been fortunate to have people in my life who've held a space for me to explore ideas and create new options in my professional and personal life.

Ivor Telamaque, my self-appointed mentor, continues to provide a non-judgmental ear as I plot my next moves and learn from the success and failings of many a harebrained scheme. He asks great questions and challenges my thinking. We've had many stimulating discussions and together saw this "safe space" idea develop into the manuscript it is today. My cheerleaders—Kathy Gonsalves, Leah De Souza, Akosua Dardaine, Wesley Welch, Connie Kadansky, and Leslie Ferrier-Attong—have supported me over the years as I shifted and morphed into who I am today. They inspire and encourage me to dream as they, too, chase their own visions.

Thanks to my team at Guardian General Insurance Company—Sharmila Singh, Candace Simmons, Melaine Mahabir,

Wendy Dickson, and Kendell Williams—for allowing me to tweak the safe space concept into what it has become. It is their stories, along with those of hundreds of people with whom I've worked over the years, that I honor and share in this book.

Thanks to Greenleaf Book Group for publishing this book: Hobbs Allison for saying yes to the project; Debra Englander for editing; Bryan Carroll for managing the project; Amber Hales for serving as managing editor; Neil Gonzalez for cover design; and Chelsea Richards for marketing. Special thanks to Elizabeth Brown for honing the manuscript, and to all the other behind-the-scenes staff.

I acknowledge the support of Laura Orsini for helping and teaching me about publicity. And I thank all of my silent supporters, well-wishers, endorsers, and reviewers of this book.

CONTENTS

Introduction

I n February 2013, at the inaugural International Association of
Facilitators conference in Jamaica, I was a last-minute addition to a panel discussion. The moderator posed the same two
questions to each panelist: "How does your company use facilitation?" And "What impact did it make?" I was truly eager to
answer these questions.

Six months before the conference, I had accepted an executive management position at an organization with a traditional
hierarchical organizational structure. Before that job, I'd worked
as a contractor, strategically avoiding leadership or managerial
roles. When I accepted the new in-house position, however, I
consciously decided I would become a particular type of leader,
not just a manager.

I was a recent graduate of Fielding University's Certified
Evidence Based Coaching program, and had experienced the

magic of coaching clients. I had also facilitated several workshops and knew the power of asking the right open-ended questions. I firmly believed that these two skill sets—coaching and facilitation—belonged in my leadership tool kit.

In that panel discussion in Jamaica, I explained the term "safe space" from both the coaching and facilitation viewpoint, and described how my team and I set it up. I described how, within six months, my office had become a place to cry, vent, question authority, challenge decisions, take risks, and most importantly, discover answers.

After the panel discussion, I received kudos on my presentation. Some members of the audience wanted to further the safe space discussions, while others asked if I offered training courses and a few even asked if I was hiring. There seemed to be a genuine interest in the concept.

At that same conference, I had the pleasure of meeting Trevor Stewart, who told me that I needed to have some fun. I had just completed my first book, Change or Die: The Business Process Improvement Manual, a management book that provides a proven how-to approach for people who want to redesign processes within their organizations.

Trevor told me he found that book dense, and suggested I write another one that would make it easy for people to relate to me and my experiences. I kept bumping into him at the conference, and he kept encouraging me to think about that second book. We were at the airport when I made the final commitment to write a second book.

Unlike my first book, the book you're reading is not a how-to book. There are no tables and no workshops. I lovingly refer to

Change or Die as my "head book," where I wrote about everything involved in "process improvement." This book, *Lead Your Team to Win: Achieve Optimal Performance by Providing a Safe Space for Employees*, is written from my heart, and speaks of the challenges and failures that led me to create a new style of managing people. It's a book about what has worked for me. Though I continue to learn more every day, I encourage you to try some of these strategies. And of course if you have any questions, please feel free to drop me a line.

What Is a Safe Space?

Imagine that you are in the office, with a pile of work on your desk. Although your head is not there today, you have shown up because you have some pending deadlines. Perhaps your dog died, you had a major fight with a loved one, or a coworker is stressing you out. Try as you might to ignore your personal issues, they just keep popping up, affecting your ability to concentrate and slowing down your pace of work. What would it be like if you could go into a room where you have total support and have a good cry for the dead dog, vent how angry you are at your loved one, or rant about how stressed you are over the coworker's behavior? When you are done, you leave the room knowing that your behavior was not judged and that anything you said was confidential. You return to your desk and comfortably resume working.

Or suppose you are sitting in a meeting and get this brilliant idea you believe might solve a major problem for the company. You can't share it in the meeting because you don't have all the pieces yet, but your gut says you are onto something big. You enter an office and chat with someone who will not steal your idea. This person helps you work out the concept and weigh the options until you're crystal clear about the way forward. You then write up and present your idea, certain that you'll get full credit for it.

Or say that you are on your third cup of coffee and you just can't seem to settle down. You've been procrastinating completing a critical task. Success means a huge bonus, and messing up is not an option. Rather than remaining in anxiety mode, you get help identifying the risks and working out mitigation plans. You work past the fear, knowing that even if you fail at the task you will probably learn something new. And you'll still have the opportunity to try again, to succeed, and to have another shot at that bonus.

The safe space allows each of these and many other scenarios to play out. It's a place for you to release emotions and get past negative feelings, to shift the issues that bother you so you can pay closer attention to your work. It's where you create clarity in life's confusing moments, and park the problems that inhibit your performance. It provides room for you to take risks that lead to rewards.

A safe space is one of no judgment. It is a space where you can cry, curse, and get rid of what's on your chest. It's a retreat where you can say that you are overwhelmed and rest for a few minutes before you resume work. It's a place where you can release the emotional, stressful stuff that wears you down and keeps you stuck.

A safe space is the office Vegas: what happens in the room stays in the room. This is the place to be weak, vulnerable, indolent, petulant, and indulgent, knowing that whatever is said and done happens in a pre-arranged place that won't haunt you or result in repercussions down the road. You can always leave with your dignity intact.

This is not an advice-giving space or a counseling session. It's a container for holding negative emotions. It's a clearinghouse that allows good feelings to emerge and bad feelings to subside. It shifts the balance between what is real and unreal, between fear and courage, between anxieties about the future and needs of the present—to restore equilibrium and inner peace. It is a physical space that allows you some mental space. It's where you go to clear your mind so you can return to work with greater focus.

The safe space is also for dreaming. Employees imagine how they want the organization to look and feel, and then plot projects to make it happen. It is the space for the impossible to become possible. It is the team's think tank, the place for risk taking. In here the leader may prompt the team to be ridiculous, to go for big ideas. Though people might come in believing that failure is an option, they will leave with the confidence to try something new, and—if necessary—the permission to fail.

The safe space is designed for exploring organizational issues, challenging the status quo, asking questions, and creating solutions. This is the place for effective planning, fine-tuning details, and making decisions. It is where workers are offered the space to prepare: for the big meeting, difficult presentation, worrisome job interview, or other career-changing moments.

It is a place that supports the team to work at its optimum

and removes the obstacles that may hinder progress. The safe space recognizes that between the desired outcome and the current realities are personal and professional debris that need to be cleaned up before the job can be done. Team members are encouraged to drop their burdens, those personal and professional issues that keep them up at night and prevent them from doing their best work.

Usually we can compartmentalize, and keep our work and personal lives separate; but there are times when the walls between the two break down. I used to pride myself on my ability to keep my private life from interfering with my work life. Each morning I locked my apartment door, securing my dreams and hopes behind, and went to work. Privately, I dreamed of being a writer, but I had an accounting career. For a long time, I focused on my job and denied my desire to write. However, one day my need to write became greater than the need for the steady income that accounting provided, and I became resentful of my profession, even though I was well paid and enjoyed a good life. I was no longer proud of my accounting qualifications; my accomplishments seemed fake and false. I could feel the walls between my two lives cracking. My inability to reconcile my personal desire (to write) with the reality of my professional life (as an accountant) left me claustrophobic, and the struggle took a personal toll. On the outside I had a great life; but inside I was in turmoil. I was ill equipped to deal with this internal conflict, and my ability to work was compromised. Yet, I was expected to show up every day and perform.

Looking back, I know now that if I could have found a way to marry my passion for writing with my accounting job, then I could have found a resolution. If I'd had a space that I could have used to clear my head, as well as someone to listen to my story of struggle, I may have gained enough clarity to continue to hold my accounting position and also write. But I didn't have such a space, and never found such a solution.

I know that many team members are just like I was, trying to balance private ambitions with work demands. And I know how difficult it is to maintain that balance. The safe space encourages team members to reconcile their personal and work lives by bringing their ambitions and dreams to the office. In the space, we learn that there is no need to sever this most sacred part of ourselves—the private dreams—in order to work. Rather, we're encouraged to use our creativity and intelligence in our work. The safe space allows us to honor all of who we are, every single day.

My office these days is a safe space where coworkers can think, emote, plan, and take risks. When a team member wants my ear, my role is to keep the member feeling safe, limit the distractions, and keep him company while he gets rid of negative feelings, thus creating a vacuum for better feelings to rush in and fill. I am very clear that I cannot and will not act on what is said, unless of course my colleague threatens harm to himself or someone else.

The safe space transforms my office for a few moments into a magical and powerful place. People come into the room to speak about personal and professional successes and failures. They have "aha" moments, question decisions, state fears, shake their heads, laugh, shout, and cry. They learn about themselves, and what makes people tick. It is a place to experience the personal growth that fuels professional development and celebrates both the private and public achievements that are important to each of us. It is a place of discovery and wonder that allows visitors to see life from a different perspective. In the safe space anything can happen and there is nothing to fear.

How does this safe space operate? When a member needs to vent, you let her vent. Do not defend the issue she may be upset about; nor do you want to pacify her. Just observe and say nothing. When a member needs to cry, let him cry; offer a tissue and leave him alone. Maintain physical distance; do not touch him, hug him, or pat his back. It is not your role to soothe or to stop the tears. Let team members rant, laugh, and express how they feel about the issues they are dealing with. I am not a counselor; I do not know the root cause of the emotion, nor do I try to stop the emotion. I let it flow; I am present, attentive, and aware of the members as they express themselves.

I use the safe space as well, and call on my team members to support me. When my CEO rejected a project that I submitted, I shared my feelings with the team. This helped me get over my disappointment and indicated to members that I know how they feel in similar situations. In the safe space we realize that nothing is really too big, that the way we feel is not unique, and that we all struggle with something. The space allows us to support each other's humanity so we can get on with the important tasks at hand.

CONCLUSION

Once a safe space has been established in an office, and workers have become accustomed to knowing such a non-judgmental space is always available to them, the concept can extend to other areas. This has happened in my workplace: my safe space has extended beyond my office walls. Fellow team members have created safe spaces for each other in their cubicles and in the areas where they sit. They provide space for each other to question, to share doubts, and to vent. The concept has reached beyond a physical space and has become the way we treat each other. We hold this sacred space ready wherever and whenever our team members need it.

The safe space benefits both the team leader and the members. Team members are then able to get on with the work at hand, and the leader is assured that work is getting done.

Why a Safe Space?

Although I have been a manager since age twenty-five, I haven't always liked it. I thought that being a good manager meant doing all the work, fixing everything that was broken, supporting team members through their personal breakups, divorces, ill kids, marriage, anxieties, etc. Back then, I went home every day juggling all this new and unwanted information about my colleagues. Soon I found that telling people what to do, having to always be right, taking responsibility for other people, taking initiative with limited authority, and fixing other people's messes were absolutely exhausting.

I was taught that to be a good leader, I needed to be strong, and never appear weak. I needed to be even-tempered and rational, giving an excellent performance regardless of my personal problems. Unfortunately, maintaining this demeanor is difficult for me. It is hard for me to pretend that I am not upset, mad, disappointed, shocked, or hurt. I simply cannot accept the notion that I can automatically function at the top of my game at all times.

I wanted a leadership style that would work with my personality and still allow me to have a winning team. I knew that creating a safe space in my office was essential to achieving this since it would:

- Get people to work creatively and generate ideas and new solutions.

- Develop an incredible team with outstanding performance that ensured me, as the leader, promotions and wins. (My assumption is that each time a team member wins, the leader automatically gets one or two wins.) To achieve wins, team members must have big ideas and the guts to implement them. They need to fail and believe that while there's a cost to failure, there's no personal loss; and they can certainly try again. To win, the team needs to work together, think strategically about their actions, and always weigh consequences. The safe space provides a cocoon in which ideas are hatched, nurtured, and grown before being released to a wider audience for scrutiny.

- Provide a stable environment in which everyone can perform, even on the days when nothing seems to go right.

- Allow team members to bring to work the adult parts of themselves that they often park at the office door and retrieve when they leave the office. This safe space gives them permission to be the responsible, accountable, decision-making, trying-to-be the-best-they-could-be people they are outside of the office. These people make tough decisions every day about household budgets, their children's future, and aging parents. They fail and keep going, juggling different balls to keep their lives and those of their loved ones on an even keel.

- Permit team members to think, and in so doing challenge me to think more. They need to ask questions so I can explain and become clearer, and thus we can all generate even more great ideas and make better decisions.

- Motivate the team so people feel good about what they are doing, and work well because of these positive feelings. When the team members feel safe, they'll take risks that will bring rewards, and will accept challenges to grow professionally and personally.

- Keep my big ego in check, ensuring that my natural tendencies to be a benevolent autocrat don't overtake my humanity. This keeps me honest and responsible for the things I do and say at the office. It also gives me the freedom to change my mind and not be seen as indecisive, and releases me from the burden of feeling I always have to be right.

- Satisfy my curiosity about leadership and the many strategies I've read about. I wanted to create an alternative style that would work with my personality and allow me to remain true to myself. I wanted to present an alternate and realistic tool that people like me could easily implement with their teams.

The safe space provides a dynamic and creative environment for the free exchange of ideas, and encourages team members to make decisions and take action. While it promotes team accountability, it does not release the leader from the ultimate responsibility for making the final decisions. The idea promotes a shared team consciousness about the reality of the bigger political landscape within which the team operates, and dissuades any pretensions of naïvety about how the organization and various stakeholders need to be maneuvered. Thus, it provides a reality check for the team and its members.

The safe space means that I do not have to coddle or barter for good performance. I do not have to instruct the team to subscribe to some abstract premise, nor do I have to make any promises that I may not live up to. The safe space works because ultimately the team and I want the same thing—to win.

Early in my career, before I had fully developed the concept, I was selected as manager to replace the newly appointed finance director. My predecessor had close but messy personal relationships with the finance team members. Suddenly, I found myself in the middle of this chaos and had to be the buffer between the director and the team members. I translated her messages and demands into palatable requests until she believed that I "got them to work" and that I "had the patience to hold their hands." The team members also communicated messages to her through me, for approvals or any special requests that only she could grant. After three years in this position, I was burned out. I loved my job, made some important changes, and was proud of my achievements. But after gaining the trust of the director and the team, while working long hours managing both parties and being solely responsible for all the decision making, I wanted out and resigned.

After that experience, I did not want any more leadership responsibility. I spent the next ten years doing contract and short-term jobs, enjoying the easy life of a contract worker—driven by deadlines and objectives. There was no one to worry about, no need to build relationships. I could just move from job to job and do the work. Or so I thought.

I was the project manager for the transfer of data from one IT platform to another. The project sponsor had set some tight deadlines and was at loggerheads with the project manager about the next steps. The project team was caught up in the maelstrom of the pair. The project was behind schedule, and the team felt that failure was imminent and nothing could stop the wreckage. I worked with the team to reset targets and deadlines, and persuaded the sponsor to create some performance incentives while I negotiated some wins for both sponsor and manager. At the end of the project, I was asked to consider taking on a more permanent position, but I declined. I had become way too involved in managerial issues and shunned the responsibility.

Project assignments provided me with lots of opportunities to observe. I worked at thriving companies that have been around for decades, and had healthy profit margins. Wherever I worked, I noticed there was an ongoing conflict that derived from an "us vs. them" attitude. It could be team members vs. team members, leaders vs. team members, leader vs. leader, manager vs. manager, but the result was the same: it prevented people from getting the job done. I also realized that because everyone wanted to be right, no one could take the chance of being wrong. There was a palpable fear of failure that delayed decision making and paralyzed teams, preventing them from taking action, while leaders initiated only those projects within their expertise to ensure success.

Save for a few companies, there was a dearth of leadership, as most leaders seemed just as bewildered as the team members. Enough work was getting done to keep the wheels turning and the trains on the track, but with very little innovation. Leaders were delegating work and covering their backs when things went wrong, and members were playing it safe by doing as their leaders said and nothing more.

When my colleague Beatrice was promoted to finance director, she worked as if she was on her own. Without the support of her team, she initiated and implemented projects, made exceptional contributions to the organization, and worked long hours—often to the detriment of her personal life. Beatrice received huge annual bonuses and hefty salary increases, while the rest of her team members remained more or less at their entry-level salaries. She was winning and her team was losing. Her team felt betrayed and resented her success. Members began to view her as a selfish liar, since she did not make good on the silent expectation that the team would move ahead together. Instead, she had taken care of herself, gotten promoted, and left them behind. The team grew mistrustful of the entire management team, since an irresponsible leader had been promoted and the team's contributions to her success went unnoticed. They retaliated by doing exactly what they were told, completing only their "literal" job descriptions.

Meanwhile, Beatrice knew that her team members had the qualifications for their jobs but thought they were lazy and lacked initiative. In fact, she wanted to get rid of the entire team.

This scenario is often played out in many companies. A manager is promoted but the team members are not; they grow resentful, while remaining uncertain about how to improve things. They cannot articulate what they want, so they're unable to ask for help. Instead, they become frustrated, annoyed, and silently withdraw from the organization. They may be showing up every day, but they're no longer contributing all they have to the company. The lucky ones move on to organizations where they receive better support, but the majority stay, with no achievements to put on their resumes, performing just enough not to be fired. No one tells them how to get out of the rut, or provides the guidance needed to move ahead. The employees remain in task-oriented roles and refer all decisions upward. They do not perceive any alignment between their tasks and the organization's vision. They neither expect nor deserve promotions; they neither win nor lose. Instead, they remain in a neutral position, flying just below the organizational radar.

I went back into management for selfish reasons. After realizing the importance of reconciling my personal life with my professional life, I developed expertise in strategy, facilitation, and coaching, which were a better fit for me than accounting. I wanted to put these skills to work in an organizational setting, which meant returning to a traditional environment, although I had found leading people difficult in the past.

I was clear about the type of leader I wanted to be. As a facilitator, I knew how to lead a group to consensus and generate commitment to that decision. As a coach, I've learned that people always have an answer to the issues they face, and my responsibility is to help them unearth that truth. Both practices propose that clients need to feel safe so they can speak, question, state concerns, and challenge the status quo to move forward. I concluded that these techniques could be used in the office to create a safe space for team members to think, gain clarity, and reassess the challenges they face each day.

CONCLUSION

I created the safe space so team members could get past the fear of failing—so they could make decisions and take risks. I created a safe space for my team members so they could be seen and heard—to know their thoughts are valued and they have the potential to make positive contributions to the organization. I created the safe space so members could integrate their personal and professional lives, rather than carry resentment toward their work when personal issues crop up. This way the team isn't held back by one member who has unresolved personal issues; and thus all team members can excel.

Creating the safe space has not been easy. People are weary of "leadership jargon," and their past experiences make them skeptical of change. However, employees began to show interest in the safe space when they heard it was a way for them to get ahead and win. My team gingerly joined the experiment and after seeing the benefits, they actively began to participate in keeping the space safe.

The space allowed me to co-create a collaborative partnership with team members and share collective responsibility for the successes and failures of the team. This ensures two key things: that I don't suffer burnout from carrying the weight of my team; and in my desire to move ahead, I don't leave the team behind.

How It Works

As mentioned in Chapter 2, the safe space draws on principles and practices used in coaching and facilitation. Both disciplines promote the theory that the client needs to feel safe in the non-judgmental environment provided by the coach and/or facilitator. The coach or facilitator acts as a neutral third party who does not have a vested interest in the outcome. This person leads the client to discover and take responsibility for whatever the client wants to achieve. The safe space leadership style is based on three common psychological theories that underpin both coaching and facilitation. These are explained briefly in the following pages.

Before I explain the psychology, however, you might equate the safe space to the techniques used in religion, addiction recovery programs, therapeutic counseling, or coaching. This one-on-one interaction between the "patient" and the non-judgmental coach, priest, or therapist works because the patient isn't told what to do. Instead, the confessor listens and asks questions designed to help lead the client to recovery. The interactions between the confessor and the client happen in a safe space, where the client can say whatever he wants, knowing that it remains confidential; and he leaves knowing he has acknowledged, made amends, repented, and left his burdens behind. Much of the same work occurs in the safe space: we acknowledge that we have a problem, a fear, a concern, or something that is preventing us from completing and moving forward with our work. In fact, sometimes simply stating this reality is enough to get us moving again.

Safe space draws on the principles of:

- **Carl Rogers** (1902–1987) Creator of humanistic psychology

  Carl Rogers developed a client-centered or non-directive approach to his clients. He disagreed with the generally accepted view of his time that the therapist knew more about the client or had a better understanding of the client's problems. Instead, he saw the relationship between the therapist and the client as collaborative, with the therapist paying attention to the client's state of mind and asking questions designed to help the client resolve issues. Rogers thought people had the capacity to grow, could solve their own problems, and would do what ultimately is good for them.

  My own understanding of the safe space is built on the positive assumptions that members have the intelligence and creativity to solve their own problems. The leader is asked to trust that the team members can and want to solve problems. In a collaborative relationship, both leader and team members create the working agenda and determine what works best for the team.

- **Malcolm Knowles** (1913–1997) Identified adult learning

  Knowles believed that as a person matures, his self-concept moves from being dependent toward being a self-directed human. As such, the adult becomes more interested in self-developmental tasks and his own societal roles. The adult wants to learn what is relevant to his immediate needs and wants to apply these immediately; he/she is not interested in abstract learning but instead wants to learn something that will solve problems. Knowles explained the motivation behind adult learning with the following six assumptions. Knowles's assumptions also explain why the safe space works and identify how team members are to be engaged.

Assumption 1: Adults need to know the reason for learning. The purpose of the safe space and how it works needs to be explained to the members so they will understand how the space will work for them. With this understanding, they can then adapt to the new style of learning.

Assumption 2: *Adults prefer to be self-directing and want to be in control of their learning.*

To accomplish this, the leader needs to give team members the freedom to make choices about work with necessary levels of responsibility and authority. When members choose the projects they are interested in and determine how they will execute them, they in turn feel they have control over their jobs. This increased level of decision making allows them to take charge of their professional lives and to select the experiences that are relevant to their personal and professional development.

Assumption 3: *Adult life experiences provide rich resources for learning.*

Members have valuable experiences and skills they don't utilize at work. Leaders should encourage team members to apply these "life" skills at work and explore these experiences to further motivate them to do their work. Helping members reflect on both failings and successes helps them to learn from their experiences. Exploring personal issues in the safe space also helps members understand there is no true separation between personal and work life.

Assumption 4: *Adults learn to solve real life problems.*

In the space, the leader encourages inquiry and exploration of different ideas. Asking "what" and "how" questions will help members solve problems both as a team and as individuals.

Assumption 5: *Adults are interested in practical application of what they've learned.*
Adults want to know how what they learn relates to what they want to achieve. Ideally the members should feel that whatever happens in the space will enable them to improve the quality and output of their work. Members are given leadership opportunities as they work within and outside the team. The members' overall career goals can also be aligned to the discussions in the safe space.

Assumption 6: *Adults are self-motivated.*
When all team members agree that the objective of the safe space is for them to win, then it's easier for the leader to make assignments since everyone is aiming for the same winning result. Team members see tasks as getting them closer to the overall objectives and are self-motivated as they take responsibility for their own personal and professional development.

- **Neuroplasticity**, also known as brain plasticity

   In the early 20th century, neuroscientists thought the brain structure couldn't be changed after early childhood. Recent findings challenge that; this new thinking is called neuroplasticity, and it explores how the brain changes throughout life. The brain is now seen as malleable as it continues to reorganize itself and build new neural connections, which suggests that people can continue learning and adjusting to new situations as they present themselves.

In the safe space, team members all have the capability to learn new things and build new habits to replace the old ones that no longer serve them.

In all, these three theories provide a rationale for why the safe space works.

CONCLUSION

The "code" of the safe space means that each member is seen and heard without judgment or repercussion. Everyone is equal among colleagues and peers. The team members bring their "adult" selves to work together to co-create and maintain the space. The space assumes that the adults in the room want to be in charge of their lives and want to have relevant work experiences that contribute to their overall goals

Make the Choice

You've probably attended a lecture, read a book, or heard about some new research and thought, "Yes. This is what we need in the office." When you hear about a concept that promises benefits, you want to introduce other people to it so that everyone can reap the potential rewards. In the first week, we share the idea with everyone and seemingly everyone is excited by the new idea. During the second week, some people start asking questions about how to implement the steps and what they mean. By week three, the team gets tired of trying to figure out "everything" and by week four, the team accepts defeat and slowly the idea ebbs away until no one mentions it again.

To implement the concept of the safe space, you must first understand and be able to convey what it is and why you are doing it. The safe space is about creating an environment in which your team feels secure enough to take risks. The safe space is about making each member of your team a winner so that in turn you, the leader, can win. You must fully understand the what, the why, and the how of the space before you introduce it to your team.

To get started, you should call your team together and explain that you have an innovative idea you want to discuss. You can create a PowerPoint presentation or short document explaining the concept and highlight the potential benefits. Depending on how you interact with your team, you might have individual conversations with your colleagues since some people may be more comfortable voicing their opinions with you alone, rather than in a group.

If you're a leader, you can champion the idea and work with your team to implement the space. If you're not the team leader, then perhaps you can influence your leader to create the safe space. If the leader is not interested in the idea, you can modify the concept to create the safe space among your peers. Either way, this is not an idea that you can coerce other people to adopt. If you're the leader of the team and you're implementing the concept, then you first must assess whether you and your team are ready. Your current relationship and history with your team will determine how you approach implementation.

NEW LEADER

If you've just joined a department as manager, it will probably be easy for you to introduce and implement the safe area since you have no history with the team. When I was in this position and told my team about my concept, the staffers were very curious. I told them how I wanted to work and why I wanted to work with them this way. We met frequently on the topic and kept distilling the idea until everyone was comfortable with it. I explained how the concept was to be set up and encouraged feedback from members. They asked questions and developed scenarios, challenging the specifics of the concept. I answered the questions as best as I could, admitting when I didn't have an answer. As we set up the space, we continuously reset boundaries, renegotiated rules, and worked through issues until we had consensus. Most importantly, I had to demonstrate the type of behavior I wanted in the room and stay open to every discussion without making judgments on the discussions.

Since the space called for personal responsibility and challenged the members to do more than they were currently doing, I had to be very patient and listen to a lot of "that is not the way we do things" as members expressed disbelief and discomfort with their new levels of authority and responsibility for making decisions.

The finance team also used the space, although its implementation took longer because the team distrusted management. This team was encouraged to focus on the rationale of the process, not the leader, to determine whether it could work for them. Once the employees understood the concept, they turned their attention to me and my behavior. When they saw I was consistent and fair in how I worked with team members, they gradually warmed to the concept. I had to prove myself as trustworthy and responsible for the team and its efforts before they could trust me and, by extension, the space.

EXISTING LEADER WITH GOOD RELATIONSHIP

If you have a great relationship with your team members and they trust your leadership, then the safe space becomes a welcome addition to your management tool kit. The idea is easy to implement since the trust that your team has in you is the foundation on which the idea will be built. Team members will rally around the space and willingly participate as they do with most of your ideas. Any misconceptions that arise will be worked out easily, and this team is ready for the safe space.

EXISTING TEAM WITH POOR RELATIONSHIP

The leader of the team was startled. Her ten team members started work at 7:30 each morning and it was now 7:45. She received calls from six people, each one saying he or she had food poisoning and would not be coming to work. By 8:00, she was furious. All the team members had called to say they had the same ailment; no one was coming in. The next day, one of the employees actually boasted that everyone had skipped work to go to the beach.

Why would a group of people jeopardize their jobs, performance ratings, bonuses, and potential salary increases to defy a leader? If all of the team members are willing to forgo benefits to defy the leader, then they are involved in a toxic relationship. The office has become a battlefield with both leader and members winning small conflicts while neither party advances, since in the long run, neither the team nor the leader wins. The entire team is viewed as a problem by the rest of the organization, which feeds into the ill feelings that exist with the team. In this scenario, the team members did not trust the leader and the leader returned the favor by micromanaging the team and taking them to task for mistakes. The leader complained about the team members and the team members retaliated whenever they felt they'd had enough. This team underperformed, had high absenteeism, and high turnover. The leader needed to salvage her career; she had already been turned down for an internal transfer because she could not successfully manage her current team. She wanted to adopt the safe space so that she could win. She admitted that team members were not going to readily embrace the concept, since her relationship with the team was already so shaky. She knew that the team needed several honest conversations before they could begin to use the word safe.

A skilled facilitator, who was a neutral third party, was brought in to lead a series of meetings to deal with the outstanding issues. The facilitator ensured that everyone felt safe, each person was seen and heard, and there was no judgment in the room. The team vented about events and issues and came to agreement on how to resolve these issues and limit their reoccurrence.

The facilitator then focused on the level of trust in the room and worked with the team members to develop a list of behaviors they considered safe and unsafe. The team continued to have monthly facilitated meetings to compare displayed behaviors to the list of agreed behaviors and determine which of these actions eroded or built trust. Over time, the team agreed that the level of trust in the team was increasing, and they met less frequently as the facilitator continued to gauge the trust in the room.

The team leader took the comments heard at the meetings, and actively demonstrated that she understood her role in creating the problems with the team. She worked with a coach to limit her behaviors that decreased the levels of trust and increased those that built trust. There was no discussion about developing a safe space until trust was established between the members and the team leader.

Eventually, the facilitator invited the team and leader to co-create a working environment that would mimic how they felt in the facilitated meetings and would lead to openness and lack of judgment, while allowing issues to be successfully handled. The team members were eager to extend the safety they experienced in the facilitated meetings to the office environment since they understood how it could benefit their work on a daily basis. The leader continued the coaching sessions and invited the facilitator to lead team-building exercises for the team from time to time.

The changes the leader incorporated into her behavior were essential to the team's embrace of the safe space. When she demonstrated behaviors that kept the space safe, then members developed trust and gave the space a chance. If she had refused to change her conduct and did not make amends for her slips, the safe space would not have been implemented. The team may trust the process, but they won't have confidence in the space if they have a leader who cannot be trusted.

If you and your team have any outstanding issues, work on these first to get the team to a more neutral position before implementing the safe space. If you can't do this, then you need to be prepared for a long and slow introduction period, or an eventual rejection of the concept.

PERSONAL INVENTORY

Leaders need to do some self-examination to determine if they can set up and maintain the safe space. When I was ego driven and everything was about me, then I could not work with the safe space. I made decisions that propelled my personal success and made me look good. I had little interest in what worked for the team. It is easy to spot ego thinking like I exhibited. You are making an ego decision whenever you think, "What would others think about me?" or "What does this say about me?" or "How will I look?" These questions center only on the leader and the decisions are often about saving face. To deflect the thinking from oneself and extend it outward toward the team members, the leader needs to ask, "How does this work for the team?" or "How does this advance the goals of the team?" or "How does this impact the safety of the space?" before making decisions and taking actions. If the answers suggest that the decisions or actions may negatively impact the team or compromise the safety of the space, then the leader can delay taking action until she or he can devise another plan that will positively impact the team.

Scenario analysis can also help with this by asking, "What will happen to the space if I do Y?" If the leader cannot do this, then she can bounce ideas off one of the team members who will quickly set the record straight.

When I thought I was the only intelligent voice in the room,

I could not set up the safe space. I was an upcoming accountant with all the qualifications, and I thought no one else could contribute to my thought process. After all, I was the most creative person, the one with all the bright ideas, and I knew the answer to everything. This attitude suffocated team members and forced my way of thinking on them. Consequently, there was no sharing of ideas, no openness, and the room was not safe.

When I was impatient and wanted to solve problems immediately, I asked closed-ended questions that suggested I knew all the answers and only wanted confirmation of my brilliance. Asking open-ended questions helped me to lessen this impulse as I bit my tongue and gave others a chance to think and state their opinions.

When I wanted to get everything right as if work were an exam, the space was not safe. I would be angry when people made mistakes; I would even have a mini-tantrum if I didn't catch an error before the work reached my superiors. When I learned that mistakes have value as learning tools, I treasured and sought the lessons they held.

When I was solely focused on the results by any means necessary, the space could not be safe. I worked long hours every day and clocked over 24 continuous work hours at the office on more than one weekend, bringing in projects with impossible deadlines on time. My motto was "If I could do it, the team can do it." I drove myself and my team to great results, ignoring the personal sacrifices required to do so. There was no balance between work and personal life. Work was my only priority. Neither my team members nor I were safe as I relentlessly drove us to success without giving any thought to our non-work lives.

At times, I was emotionally unaware of my behavior and

what drove it. My behavior may have been triggered by ancient incidents and I occasionally reacted completely inappropriately. Consequently, the space was not a safe place. Since then, I have learned what my emotional triggers are and how to separate the present from the past. I have learned to behave appropriately in a professional setting and manage my personal feelings in a way that allows the space to remain safe for everyone.

As I learned more about myself and how my reactions affected other people, I was able to evaluate my behavior and change some of my behavioral patterns. By reading, consulting, coaching, and working with a counselor, I changed my management style to one that is more supportive of my colleagues and focuses on helping them succeed.

Leaders need to take a personal inventory of our behavior and the things we say and do. We need to be honest and ask ourselves if we can keep the space safe. We can then work to change the things about ourselves that may make the space unsafe. If we are unaware of our actions and the effect they have on others, then we need to ask for feedback from the team or peers. If we are unwilling to become safe people, then we have to admit we cannot create a safe space.

The safe space will not work if your management style is one of manipulation or coercion, if you lead by fear, or if you pit team members against each other. For a safe space to succeed, you must have a management style that focuses on building a collaborative team by being a fair, honest, and trustworthy team leader. The team does not have to fear, worship, or even like you, but the members need to be able to trust that the space is stable and that it allows them to perform.

We all have personal biases that cause us to disapprove of the way someone dresses, speaks, or acts; some people just rub us the wrong way. While nothing is inherently wrong with these feelings, leaders cannot allow them to run unchecked or they will interfere with the leader's ability to interact with her colleagues. The leader must be able to distinguish among personal feelings, biases, emotional triggers, and how these impact the way she treats team members.

A leader who thinks her alma mater churns out the best professionals needs to be aware of this bias and must ensure that she doesn't treat persons from other colleges differently from the way she treats alumni from her school. She needs to control her enthusiasm for fellow alumni in the work environment to ensure that she keeps the playing field level for all team members.

I am very aware of my personal biases and constantly question myself on what is the real issue when faced with the triggers to my biases. I check myself first to establish my role in the problem. I use the wisdom learned as a kid; when I point a finger at someone, there are three fingers pointing back at me, indicating that I am part of the problem. I then ask myself, "How did I contribute to this?" or "What are those negative feelings saying about me?" or "How am I treating the person because of my beliefs?"

I changed my behavior significantly and I keep changing as I commit to make the space safe. The list below shows some of the areas in which leaders make changes to keep the space safe for team members:

- **Leaders need to understand their level of emotional intelligence.**

- Leaders need to work on their personal development.

- Leaders need to communicate effectively.

- Leaders need to be able to say sorry or I was wrong and not have a meltdown.

- Leaders need to be able to hear a different opinion.

- Leaders need to count to ten.

- Leaders need to give members the benefit of the doubt.

- Leaders need to assume that members act from a place of good intentions.

- Leaders need to check for motive.

- Leaders need to be able to say "no" and not feel guilty.

- Leaders need to be humble.

- Leaders need a sense of humor.

- Leaders need to be able to fail.

- Leaders need to be consistent.

- Leaders need to be responsible.

- Leaders need to be honest.

- Leaders need to be trustworthy.

- **Leaders need to be fair.**

- **Leaders need to be open to suggestions.**

- **Leaders need to ask open-ended questions.**

- **Leaders need to not take themselves seriously.**

- **Leaders need to have fun with their teams.**

IT IS OK

Members will embrace the concept at different rates according to their past experiences with the leader, the organization, other team members, or life in general. The leader needs to be patient and consistently display behaviors that allow trust to be built.

Regardless of past relationships within the team, the space can be implemented, although doing so may require external assistance to bring the team and leader to a position from which they can hatch the idea. Even without external help, open and honest conversations will show whether the space is safe and what needs to be done to correct the defects.

If you are thinking the safe space requires too much of you personally and that you are not ready to provide it, then you're probably right. Implement the parts of the concept that can be easily adopted by your team.

Safe space or not, if you want to be a better leader, then you will be a better leader. If you want to lead your team well, you will keep experimenting with the ways that serve you and the needs of your team. Decide what kind of leader you want to be and how you want your team to talk and think about you. Think of the kinds of issues and the topics about which you want your team to be comfortable enough to speak to you. Your thoughts will determine the type of leader that you will be. Shift your thinking to include bigger ideas and imagine that your team wants more and that you can help them to achieve more.

CONCLUSION

By maintaining a focus on the neutral act of winning in a way that acknowledges the humanity of team members, the safe space concept can be implemented and maintained.

I never doubted that the safe space would work. I have had great results with my new team. Some of them have left the organization after learning that their personal goals were misaligned with those of the company; others have been promoted and lead other teams, while some who had been considered un-promotable became authorities in their respective fields. None of these activities would have happened without the safe space. It simply furthers the focus on producing high-quality results so the team can win.

I am resolute about my commitment to the space. I believe in the principles of the space and continually stress that it's for the members to own and use. As new employees and teams use it, they also understand it is designed to benefit the individual and the team as a whole.

Your team members are creative and intelligent and want to make a difference. You can give them the permission they need to do this. Embracing this concept will enable you to shift your leadership style, which will further your own goals and ultimately benefit your team's performance.

The Concept of Caring

Performance evaluations were due to the human resources (HR) department by March 30. The cycle was the same every year and reminders were sent out in January. It was now the end of February and none of the team members had set a date for discussing their reviews. At the next weekly meeting I declared, "In full disclosure, my performance evaluation was signed off by the CEO and submitted to HR."

They looked at me puzzled, until one of them piped up, "Why didn't you remind us about ours?"

I counted to ten and said, "That is not my responsibility. I care about my performance evaluation so I got mine done. You do not seem to care about yours." They left my office shocked.

I understood my team members' shock. For the last six months, we had been building our safe space and they knew I wanted them to succeed. Therefore, they couldn't understand my lack of concern that they hadn't completed their evaluations. But this is not the leader's role; the leader cannot treat the members like children when it's convenient to the members, reminding them of deadlines and responsibilities.

Team members need to decide if they will abide by the rules of the evaluation process. My role is not to coerce or chase after them; this would be inconsistent to my treatment of them. Just as they choose what they want to work on each day, they need to determine what aspects of company policy they will follow. I have a vested interest in getting a bonus and a salary increase so I go to my CEO and do my evaluation. If members do not show any interest in receiving a bonus, am I supposed to encourage them to do so? In fact, the responsibility is a shared one. The responsibility for following up and making sure that tasks get done is not mine alone.

For me, the concept of the leader being a caring person is a sticky topic. I think the word care has now become a nebulous catchall for a slew of fuzzy feelings, and has been abused by both leaders and members to account for unreasonable expectations and unacceptable behaviors. Whenever I am in doubt, I look for evidence to determine the way forward. Oxforddictionaries.com defines the noun *care* as "the provision of what is necessary for the health, welfare, maintenance, and protection of someone or something."

This I understand as an obligation that the organization and its agents have for the members—the people who work and others who come into contact with the organization on a daily basis. Legal, statutory, and industry-specific requirements of doing business, coupled with the high costs of failure to comply and litigation, have led organizations to pay great attention to workplace safety for employees, clients, and anyone who may visit their physical locations.

However, other than abiding by specific workplace requirements, I am not responsible for the health, welfare, maintenance, and protection of my team members. I need to respect that my team members are adults who can provide this "care" for themselves. To think otherwise is to dishonor them.

Oxforddictionaries.com also defines the verb or action behind the word care as "feel concern or interest; attach importance to something . . . look after and provide for the needs of."

I am interested in and want team members to achieve their highest potential; after all, that is why the safe space was set up. The space is about performance since it provides members the protection to take risks. I will provide the members with guidance regarding work-related objectives and provide whatever they need to move forward, which may at times involve listening to information about their personal lives. However, I attach no importance to what the members want. One member's desires are no more or less important than another's. I am not vested in the outcome; I am a neutral third party who provides a vehicle for them to move forward. When I say that I care for team members, I mean that I am interested in them, concerned for them, and provide the tools for them to achieve their personal ambitions while balancing these with the organization's needs. I am clear that the boundaries for this care do not allow me to be involved in their personal lives.

My basic assumptions about people are that we are all innately intelligent and creative and that we strive to do better. Therefore, I treat people as I want to be treated. We can look at this another way. Do my team members care about me? Do they care if I have problems or if I cannot pay my mortgage? No, they do not and they should not. They care, in that they are interested in the impact my personal life will have on my ability to be an effective leader, but they do not care or feel concern about the effects that these situations have on me. Again, that's why I find it important to be precise in defining the way leaders "care" about team members. My personal interest is in achieving spectacular work results by maintaining the dignity and humanity of my team members. This means I am polite, empathetic, and occasionally ask about their well-being, but I don't need to be their friend.

Team members care and are interested in getting their work done, being recognized by the leader and their peers, getting a raise or promotion, and receiving the annual bonus. They don't care if their leaders fail at assigned tasks; they care whether the leader shows them how to win and navigate the organization well enough to make winning possible.

Team members are adults who have different responsibilities and challenges. They want the leader to understand that they have personal needs, which occasionally translates to the need for down time. When a team member has an emergency, he is able to take time off. Members are encouraged to stay at home when they, or family members, are ill or if they're handling a situation that would impact their ability to come into the office and work. On the other hand, the office can also provide refuge when the rest of someone's life is unstable. These decisions are acts of compassion and empathy because as human beings that is what we deserve.

In the transaction, members take from me what they need to get the job done and in exchange I ask that the work be done to particular standards. It may sound cold, but I'm being honest. Together, we set the rules of engagement and follow them to maintain the balance in the work relationship. We need to be honest and open so we can discuss, disagree, and go our own way. We need a space to cry and to pout, to shout and to rage, but we do not need someone to provide a warm and open embrace at the office.

I expect nothing from my team members except for them to complete their work. I don't want a Christmas gift, a birthday card, or an aspirin for my headache. If I get any of these, I am truly grateful and gracious when I accept, but I don't have to return the favor. I don't expect caring gestures because while they're nice to receive, they're not a required part of the team member's job. As humans we want to belong to a group and to be treated in a particular way; and we naturally develop caring feelings for each other. Leaders and members need to respect that this level of true caring is a function of time, shared experiences, and emotional connections, but it is not imperative in order for the team to work effectively together.

When leaders make a conscientious decision to care for team members, I become concerned. This should be a natural feeling and not one that needs to be declared. When leaders actively pursue opportunities to care for team members, it can lead to paternalistic behavior; likewise, members may come to expect maternalistic care from their leaders, which can result in a codependent relationship. If care does not come naturally to you as the leader, focus on what you can do. Treat members with respect and ensure that they can always, after each encounter with you, leave with their dignity intact.

PATERNALISM

Managers often have a paternalistic attitude that can create the condition: "I will take care of you if . . ." Work becomes a bargain and implies that team members should feel obliged or grateful for whatever the boss generously gives them—awards, promotions, or salary increases. It is easy to spot this attitude. You're paternalistic if you are thinking, "Team members are ungrateful," or comment, "After all that I have done," or view your team members as "selfish, not thinking of you." If you think you know what team members want without asking them or that you can speak on their behalf without their permission, then you are being paternalistic.

The relationship between leaders and team members is already unbalanced. The leader has all the power—to treat team members badly, play favorites, pit people against each other, bribe, and generally manipulate them. It is therefore very easy for a leader to be paternalistic, but this behavior doesn't help the development of the team members or the leader. Ultimately, it shows up in the work.

When leaders view their roles as promoting and protecting team members, they should think about whether they're being altruistic or expecting recognition as a payoff. When team members are promoted, get raises, or perform well, leaders have not done anything except what they should be doing. We are supposed to use our available resources to help team members navigate the organization and succeed at their jobs. While it may feed our ego when team members express gratitude, remember that the team members are the ones who did the work, and they should be congratulated on their success.

When leaders believe their knowledge or opinions are better than the team's views, then they are being paternalistic and essentially saying they can make better choices than the team. This belief is the justification for a manager telling people what they should do, taking charge of everything, and micromanaging all aspects of the work. It also allows disrespectful, demeaning, and patronizing behavior toward team members to be passed off as "in the team's interest."

It's not the leader's job to make choices for team members because the leader doesn't necessarily know what's best for the members or what choices they have made in their personal or business life. Managers overstep their boundaries whenever they delve into the personal lives of their team members such as giving advice about how to raise children or solve relationship woes. Under the guise of caring, leaders become engrossed in other people's business and cannot understand why the relationship with team members may sour. In the safe space, team members often speak about their personal lives, but I don't have subsequent conversations to find out what happened. That would be inappropriate.

Limiting my interests to the impact a personal situation may have on the team member's ability to work helps me to maintain the boundaries of the professional relationship. I keep my focus on the work and not on the lives of my team members. I don't make assumptions about their choices and I don't focus on what they should do. If a team member and I develop a relationship that mirrors a friendship—for example, if we socialize together or have equal emotional sharing about our personal lives—then the rules of engagement of how we conduct ourselves in the office will need to be renegotiated between ourselves and with other team members so there is clarity about the relationship. Until then, I maintain that the safe space is about work and I do not have to be personally interested in members' personal lives.

MATERNALISM

Team members and the wider organization often expect managers, especially female ones, to show a maternal instinct toward the team members, and nurture them. After all, some people reason that caring comes naturally to women and if it doesn't, then something must be wrong with the woman. The truth is that women don't have any better clues about managing teams than their male counterparts; both men and women have to ask the right questions. My team members are complex beings handling complex life situations. I refute the assumption that simply because I am a woman I understand them.

When leaders speak with authority about team members' behavior and link a member's personal situation to performance, those leaders are showing their maternal side. Failure to perform is often linked to something in the personal lives of the team members such as a sickly child or a troubled marriage. Interestingly, when team members perform well, no one ever makes a correlation between personal situations and work. I have yet to hear, "She is happily married; it shows in her work," or "His children are healthy, so he works well." Why then are links made between bad performance and a personal situation?

Caring for team members assumes the leader knows them and what matters to them. My team members don't know me. They don't know what I care deeply about—they build a framework from the things that I say, but they don't really know me. They don't know if I cross-dress at night, party until dawn, or create potions when I go home. My nocturnal activities are not up for discussion unless they impact negatively on my work. By extension, all discussions with team members should focus on work.

Dexter, a team leader, spent his evenings drinking copious amounts of alcohol and returned to work the next day, fully functional. It was not his leader's role to tell Dexter to stop drinking, or to point out the dangers of alcohol. The rules of engagement would allow someone to refer him to a health professional if the habit affected his work, but Dexter's work was not affected. A referral could only be based on the team leader's opinion, since there were no rules that stipulated when and how much alcohol a person could consume after work. There was no random drug or alcohol testing that could prove his work was being impacted by his alcohol consumption, so the leader could do nothing and Dexter continued drinking.

Team members and other leaders often act shocked when a leader is drunk or engages in offensive behavior at a holiday party. Remember, though, we are all human, and leaders are just as susceptible to the excesses of life. Many times leaders are forced to engage in complex deceptions because of a preference for some substance or behavior that is deemed immoral. They are expected to be more sensible, or have higher moral standards because of their roles within an organization. The leader often hides his problems and does not seek professional assistance; as a result, many capable leaders suffer unnecessary falls from grace, and are not given the empathy they need for recovery, which is an absolute pity.

CODEPENDENCY

When leaders pretend they care, they are violating the concept of the safe space by being dishonest. When team leaders and members believe they should care for each other, they establish a codependent relationship in which the parties try to take care of each other and cover or excuse the other's failings. The leader is rewarded by feeling needed, and the members have little or no choice but to become helpless in the relationship. The leader has an exaggerated sense of responsibility for the actions of members and is burdened by taking care of them. These members end up wanting to please the leader, and thus develop a constant need for approval and recognition by the leader and often feel guilty when asserting themselves. The boundaries in these relationships are blurred, as each party feels responsible for the others' feelings and problems or blames their own difficulties on another person. The leader reacts to the members' thoughts and feelings since he begins to internalize the responsibility for everyone's well-being. He believes he can fix everyone and give him or her the help they need. When members reject the help, the leader gets offended or thinks less of the members.

Leaders engaged in these relationships often fail to trust themselves or others, and may develop a compelling need to control and manipulate the teams and environments in which they operate. These leaders are often very nice as a way to exert control; when members don't reciprocate the kindness, the leaders get offended. Thoughts, feelings, and needs are often miscommunicated in this relationship, with each side pretending there are no problems. This leads to dishonesty, creates stress, and leads to destructive feelings of shame, low self-esteem, or fears of being judged or failing.

CONCLUSION

When leaders assume paternalistic relationships with the teams, they are violating the safe space. When team members look toward the leaders for maternal care, they are also violating the safe space. When any team member or leader assumes he knows what is best for others, he is setting up a codependent relationship. This behavior blurs the truth and teams then operate on a false premise that violates the safe space.

Setting Up the Space

As kids, we learned how to navigate the world and express ourselves by reading, watching TV, and listening to adults. The adults told us what to do and put words to what we felt, saw, heard, touched, or tasted. They named and explained what happened when any of our five senses was engaged. We believed that fire was hot and later we experienced what hot meant. This is generally how we learn, through a process of observation, experimentation, and teachings from those who came before us.

When I declared, "This is your safe space," I explained to the team that we could say what we thought and how we felt in the space. We could also leave the strains of our personal life in the space so that we could deal with the business of the day. This is the space where we can come to unwind and rest from the daily burdens of work and life. Here is where we can take risks and try projects without fear of failure. We can discuss, disagree, and challenge the status quo without any repercussions.

Just as we learned that fire was hot, so with the space. Team members will hear that the space is safe and will draw their own conclusions from their observations. Team members will only believe the space is safe when they experience—or see others experience—the safety of the space.

My office was assigned as the safe space since physical limitations did not allow for a separate room to be set up as the safe space. In retrospect, this was actually a good thing. Since my office was the safe space, I had to become a safe person. This meant I had to be present, aware, and mindful on a daily basis. I had to determine who I was in the office and what qualities I would display at each and every moment. I had to make a deliberate decision about how I wanted to be seen and the things that I wanted said about me. I had to be aware of the motives behind my actions and to be clear about motives in my communication as well as check that others understood my motives. I needed to be aware of my body language, my tone, and what I said. I had to hone my listening skills and pay attention to clues in the faces, expressions, and body language of the team members. This mindfulness led me to constantly evaluate and gauge my emotions to ensure my temperament and ego were in check. Being aware, mindful, and present upped the ante for me and forced me to be responsible for my thoughts, actions, and deeds.

ASSUMPTIONS

Assumptions underlie our actions and decisions. They show up in the perspective we have on life and in our belief systems. They determine how we behave and treat others. My personal assumptions tell me how I want to lead others and how I want people to engage with me.

I believe that we are all intelligent, and have the capacity to solve problems and make decisions. Our intelligence is blurred when we're scolded for talking out of turn or taught to be seen and not heard. Over time we learn that there are stupid questions and that we are foolish to ask for clarification. We learn to not seek knowledge so no one will know that we don't know, and so we stay quietly ignorant. We learn not to ask for help and pretend to know what we do not.

I believe that people are also creative and have the ability to create the lives they want. However, as children we often learn to stop being creative when we are told to grow up, be mature, and that we should no longer play with toys. When a clothing hamper stops being a place to sit and is just a receptacle for dirty clothes, and a cardboard box is no longer a rocket, we lose the ability to see things differently and think of the possibilities the world has to offer.

I also believe that people want to do better and improve their lives, which may translate to earning more, getting more responsibility, and learning something new. When we are taught that our current situation is our lot, that dreams do not come true, and that people like us—who live in our social and economic brackets and look like we do—are unable to do things differently, we accept this as our reality and lose the appetite for more.

This is my view of the world, and I offer team members the opportunity to be intelligent and creative. I suggest they can do more, and do it better than has been previously expected of them, regardless of what has already transpired. They may not share my view, but they understand the assumptions behind what I say and do. Sharing my story sets the tone for the relationship and sets my expectations.

To create your safe space, you need to determine the story behind creating the space. What are the assumptions you're making about the space, and how do you expect people to behave in it? Assumptions should be positive statements that are aligned with your personal beliefs; if they're not, it will be impossible for you to live by them every day. Team members can also be involved in creating assumptions about the space and sharing the burden of living each day with those assumptions.

MOTIVE

The important motives for setting up the safe space should be shared with the team. Stating the motives upfront allows for clarity and transparency while still opening room for discussion. When I explained my assumptions to the team, I shared that my motive was to invite each team member to bring their innate creativity and intelligence as well as their adult selves to the office on a daily basis so the team could make higher quality contributions to the organization. When I encouraged the team to conjure up ideas and projects that would make a positive difference within the organization, I explained that the motive was for the team to be recognized for the effort and for us to win. I reminded the team that I wanted to win and that this could only be achieved if the team members also won. If I was the only one bringing big ideas to the table, I would win, but if each of the team members brought an idea, then we would have five great ideas emanating from the team and we would all win. While I could win and leave the team behind, this wasn't what I wanted. I sought to create a winning team and to be a winning leader. To win, the team needs to work and work well, so ultimately this is the motive for the space. The idea of winning was something that the team could rally around and provided the motivation to give the safe space a chance.

Determine your motive for setting up the safe space and include a benefit to your team members. Adults rarely buy into a concept that promises no personal gain unless they're coerced. Your team may not agree with your motive, but they will appreciate the transparency of the idea and won't feel they have been tricked into doing something they didn't agree to do.

OWNERSHIP

Team members need to have a vested interest in the safe space. Involve the team in setting up the safe space initially so they take ownership of it from the onset. If the leader sets up the space, she is responsible for everything happening in it and the concept remains her idea.

Even though I had a clear vision of how the space should work, I invited the team to brainstorm the idea with me. Together, we created a shared concept of how it would work and understood that as the space evolved, the concept might also change. We understood that it was for individuals and the collective team. The space was ours and we were responsible for it.

RULES

Earlier in my career, I was an advocate of the open-door policy, and I allowed team members to waltz in and out of my office whenever they had something to share with me. This sharing was organic and each member had a different motive for entering the office. The safe space operates in a similar fashion, save that the space is deliberately set up with terms and conditions that governs the engagement for team members and the leader.

Everything in life has rules. There is a way to greet people, to play a game, and to cross the street. This is also true for the safe space. Rules reinforce how we behave, treat each other, and keep the space safe. The word "rules" often has a negative connotation, which would go against the spirit of the space. As a result, I rarely use the word when setting up the rules for the space.

Team members were asked to think of what they needed to be their most creative and intelligent and how they could support one another to achieve the best result. They were asked what they needed from each other to be open and feel safe in the room. Some of the questions were:

What do you need to be intelligent in the office?

What do you need to be your most creative self?

What do you need to feel safe?

What do you need to keep the space safe?

What do people need to do to keep the space safe for you?

How should people behave in the space?

What do you expect of others in the space?

What do you need to perform better in the office?

The questions deliberately focus on what the individual needs and what other people should do to fulfill these needs since we usually know exactly what our spouses, children, friends, parents, and all other people should do to make us feel better and happier. Asking questions in this way guarantees an answer by putting the onus on another person for an outcome that we want, and requires no personal commitment.

Sometimes it's easier for people to express what they do not want from a situation. If the team is stuck, pose the questions in the negative such as:

What would violate the space for you?

How would the space be violated?

What would make the space not work for you?

The answers from all the questions (positive and negative) became the rules for the space, governed the team's behavior and became the code of ethics for the team.

Over time, as people get accustomed to the space, some rules may be removed, and others may be added. Each team member signs off on the rules and receives a written copy of the signed rules.

Team members are generally good at enforcing the rules and disciplining each other when they're breaking them. New team members are introduced to the rules and given an explanation of how they are applied in various situations. People are encouraged to ask questions to ensure they understand the rules. A member who declares that she will not follow the rules still falls under the purview of my leadership and I remain responsible for her work.

She will attend team meetings and be assigned work. The other team members will be told about her choice and are asked to treat the member just as they treat each other. However, I earmark this member for transfer from my team at the earliest opportunity.

CONFIDENTIALITY

This is the most important rule for everyone. A space cannot be safe if what is said or done there is not held in confidence by each member and the leader. When Joan wanted additional time off to deal with her divorce, I extended the courtesy, and did not divulge the reasons for her absence to the other team members.

Confidentiality means the listener cannot repeat what the talker has said to anyone, including the talker, without explicit permission from the person. The listener can only break confidence if the talker plans to physically harm someone or him/herself, or to commit some other criminal offense. This limitation is explained up front so the individual is aware of the circumstances under which confidence will be broken.

The person confiding has taken a risk in sharing information; the information belongs only to that person and can be shared only by that individual. The listener was privileged to hear the information, but the information does not belong to the listener so the listener cannot share it unless given specific permission to do so. The listener can never follow up on the topic of the confidential discussion or the shared information.

The talker is free to share the information with whomever she wants, since she owns the information, with the caveat that if the talker hears the information from another source then the assumption that the listener divulged the discussion or was not confidential is false and unfair.

Most listeners understand confidentiality and do not share the content of the conversation with others but fail to appreciate that they cannot repeat the information to or follow up with the talker. We have all been embarrassed by the friend who blurts out a secret in front of a third party, or approaches us about something at an inappropriate time.

There was never a good time for me to ask Joan about her divorce because it was her personal situation. If I decided it was a good time to talk about Joan's divorce, then I would have taken ownership of the divorce and made it my business by following up on it. Joan was the only person who could decide when the time was right to speak about the divorce. It was her situation and therefore it was her decision. All I could ask was, "How are you?" and provide the opportunity for her to speak. When she answered with an "OK," I had to move on.

The talker is the only one who knows why he needs to talk about an issue at any point in time. The listener cannot assume the talker's motive; the topic may be relevant or the talker could be blowing off steam. The information shared has no value to the listener, and the listener should not hold on to it or make decisions based on it. The information given in the safe space is isolated and not connected to anything that happens in the office, unless the talker makes the connection. The listener should not link the information to behaviors, performance, or any other occurrence outside the safe space. The talker is the only one who knows the complete story, and unless the listener has asked the relevant questions and the talker given a complete explanation of cause and effect, then the listener cannot make assumptions. Any story that the listener concocts without verification from the talker is completely false.

Confidentiality between the leader and team members should to be a two-way street, but very often it is not. After team meetings with the leader, the team members often discuss what happened in the room among themselves, outside the room. When a team member has a discussion with the leader, especially if the conversation is disagreeable, that team member often discusses the exchange with his peers, while expecting the leader to hold her tongue. This may lead to tricky situations when the team member thinks the leader has divulged the information, when in reality it is another team member who has leaked the information.

Leaders therefore need to constantly remind team members of the dual obligation for confidentiality, since the responsibility for the space is shared and everyone needs to be safe in the space. Members also need to be reminded to put the onus for confidentiality on each other when they are sharing outside the space. I consider this a reality check for me as leader and expect that members will repeat things I've said, especially in an unfavorable situation. Knowing this, I have no problem with anything I say. Whatever I say to a team member I am confident that if I repeated it in front of the others, that neither the team member nor I would lose face. I do not worry, nor am I offended when members share what I said to them privately with each other, because my motive is to get the member to the other side of the situation so he or she can get back to work.

NO JUDGMENT

Passing judgment means you're ascribing a quality to a thought or a deed—whether it is good or bad, positive or negative. When team members feel their ideas will be judged, they may be reluctant to share. When the leader sets criteria for the generation of ideas (e.g., all ideas must be good), then members who lack confidence will say nothing, rather than risk having their idea judged as not being good enough.

No one sets out to make an unhelpful contribution. It is the listener who judges ideas as unwise. Team members learn that when a dumb idea is presented, the listener shares the burden of clarifying it. Perhaps the person speaking has not expressed the idea properly or the listener hasn't understood the suggestion. When we practice this way of communicating, the listener will be able to ask questions that allow the talker to develop or explain the idea further.

Ideas that sound unusual or seem out of context for the discussions at hand, when explained more clearly, often reveal different and new thinking. During a creative exercise, Stephanie selected a picture of indigenous people as representative of the team. The team members did not understand but gave her room to add context to what she meant. If the team had criticized the idea, we would have lost her brilliant contribution. When further explanation proves the idea to be irrelevant to the discussions at hand, the listener is free to reject it. But the speaker is encouraged to put forward ideas again, since he leaves knowing that the listener was genuinely interested in his contribution. When there is no judgment, everyone speaks because we all want to be heard.

When team members hold back from speaking, second-guess themselves, and make no contributions, they commit a disservice to themselves and the other team members. If Stephanie had dismissed her thoughts as ridiculous because they were different from the other perspectives, the team would not have benefited from the possibilities she shared and our discussions would have been less productive.

Team members are always encouraged to express an opinion even when "everyone has said what I wanted to say" because inevitably their thoughts are not the same. Each of us has unique experiences and ideas that add to the richness of the group's thinking. What we have to say is important and can contribute enormously to the team's thinking. It is the team's duty to help people express their thoughts.

Often a team member decides not to contribute because she assumes her thoughts are unworthy. We are often our worst critics and shut ourselves down with negative thinking. We need to stop judging ourselves so the world can benefit from our streaks of brilliance.

To get past judgment, team members are asked to be open and say what is on their mind at all times. They are also asked to accept questions as a means of helping others understand their idea, and not to be defensive when they answer. Being open gives us the freedom to question, challenge, and explain what is wrong or what is on our minds. With this freedom comes individual responsibility for how we communicate ideas and respond to other team members. The challenge is to be mindful about the impact that our judgments may have on the ability of others to feel safe.

DON'T SWEAT THE SMALL STUFF

Team members are told to assume that we are at the office to work, to produce results, and to win. This is the acid test for everything that's said and done in the office. We look at everything from this perspective and give others the benefit of the doubt that they're doing the same. This asks members to focus on the bigger picture and keep their eyes on the prize as they work. We do not let issues fester and turn into huge sores that need attention. Whenever we are offended, angry, feel slighted, or have other negative feelings, we say what we need to and move on. This releases that small irritation or negative feeling and does not let it grow. We address the feelings with the person who has offended us and not with other team members. Telling others reinforces the feelings, since each time the incident is discussed and repeated it increases our annoyance; repeating the story does not bring us relief, as the persons to whom we are complaining cannot explain the reasons behind the offender's behavior or make the necessary amends.

Not sweating the small stuff asks us to check our expectations about what is said and done by other members. We ask for clarification so that non-issues do not become issues. The small stuff finds root in rumors and gossip. When members repeat information out of context, ascribing qualities and assuming motives to what is said, small things grow into monstrous events. Not sweating the small stuff helps us to set high standards for team behavior and performance standards.

REFER TO THE LEADER

Team members need to understand that the buck always stops with the leader. The leader is the person whom the organization has vested with the power to assist them when they face problems or are in need of a solution. It is the leader who approves the projects, negotiates the politics of the organization, and at the end of the day is held accountable for what happens. When members are unsure whether they can discuss problems with each other to find solutions, they need to turn to the leader. It is the leader—and only the leader—who has the power to endorse or reject the projects, ideas, or solutions that are put forward. When the member has a problem with the leader, he needs to go to the leader. Other team members can only listen and fuel or limit the flames; the only one who can extinguish the flames is the leader. The team needs to understand this and act accordingly.

TIME TO BE SAFE

The room is always safe. The trigger for safety is switched on whenever more than one person shares the space. This applies to one-on-one or team member meetings. Team members need to be careful when they interact outside the space since they cannot assume that other members will enforce the rules outside the space. Members need to say what they want outside the space. When they want confidentiality, they need to request it and shouldn't assume that the safe space rules apply outside the safe space. Members can confirm with the other team members that they want to apply the safe space rules away from the actual safe space. This is the members' decision and does not involve the leader.

CONCLUSION

Each team develops rules that govern the way the safe space will work. Rules can be prescriptive and help people be aware of boundaries and how to stay within them. The rules are all inter-related and function together to ensure that the space remains safe. Without confidentiality, members will not say what they are thinking since they may be exposed. Without a judgment-free zone, members won't feel safe enough to speak their inner feelings.

The safe space does not work simply because the leader declares it one. Team members have to accept and agree to practice the idea; without the team, there cannot be a safe space. If the team does not agree to the idea, the leader shouldn't be discouraged. Demonstrate in the meetings and the types of discussions that are held with the team or individuals how the concept works and say that the space is available. We all have difficult days, and the first person who finds relief in the space will encourage others to follow. The safe space is an abstract concept that is only made tangible when members reap its benefits.

7

Keeping the Space Safe

Setting up the safe space is the start of the process; the work is in keeping it safe. While the team members and leaders share the duty, the leader plays a critical role in demonstrating, by the things that she does and says, that the space is indeed safe before members can truly embrace it.

The space is kept safe by giving permission for things to happen. Members feel free to ask questions, and the leader is not expected to have all the answers. No topic is too big and nothing about the organization is off limits. The leader gives the members full attention, actively listens, and limits distractions.

Leaders keep the space safe by allowing events to naturally unfold as members explore the space. The leader maintains the sanctity of the space by observing and helping the members to explore the issues raised by asking "how" and "what" questions.

The leader can use the space as well. There may be occasions when the leader uses it to express anger or feelings of being overwhelmed, or wants to bounce off an idea and get feedback from the members. When this happens, the members are maintaining the space. The space is intended for use by both members and the leader.

One day I wore an attractive blouse to work, and Shirley approached me and asked if the blouse came in her size. I was at a loss for words. She then asked, "Do you like me enough to give me that shirt?" I could not think of a response. I stood staring at her, until she moved away. I was embarrassed and fled to my office. Sarah, one of my team members, had witnessed the exchange, which heightened my embarrassment. Eventually, I called Sarah into my office and took advantage of the safe space. I recognized that I did not dislike Shirley; she reminded me of a beloved cousin who had died of a heart attack at age forty-two. I loved my cousin Dianne dearly and with Sarah's help I realized that even eight years after her death, I was still mad at her for not taking care of herself enough to prevent a fatal heart attack. My anger at my cousin was still real, and in the moment Shirley approached me, she reminded me of Dianne, since the two had similar physical appearances. I made a commitment about how to deal with Shirley in the future. In that moment, when I acknowledged the feelings that drove my silence and admitted that I was both confused by Shirley's question and embarrassed by my inability to give a suitable answer, I attained the clarity to move forward. In that instance, Sarah was the holder of the space.

I mirrored the use of the space and showed that the safe space was also a place for me to work out my issues and then get on with my job. I also showed that I was human, and that the issues didn't affect my ability to lead.

SHARING RESPONSIBILITY FOR THE SPACE

Members and leaders share responsibility for setting up the space, keeping the space safe, and providing the interaction that takes place there. Team members and leaders enforce the rules and monitor the use of the space. When members break the rules, the team discusses the problems and decides on the sanctions and steps necessary to assist the member in following the rules next time. Sharing the responsibility is not convenient. The space is kept safe by both parties involved in the transaction.

"I" STATEMENTS

In the space, we practice taking responsibility by talking from our perspective and claiming our thoughts. Speakers are discouraged from using the word "you." Instead, they must use "I." When Sandra spoke about the big project, she began, "You know when you are working on something big, and you want everything to be perfect . . ." She was stopped and encouraged to restate using "I" statements such as, "When I am working on something big, I want everything to be perfect."

Each person needs to talk about what is happening both with and to them. The member is discouraged from reporting on others or on behalf of others. This way, the member focuses on what she needs and wants out of the space. Jane cannot bring

Jack's problems into the space; Jack has to do so. She cannot take responsibility for highlighting his issues since she will be adding her opinion to the situation, which may be adding or subtracting essential information in the translation. Jane can talk about Jack only if he is directly or indirectly involved in her situation. If she wants to report on Jack, she needs to do so in his presence.

The unspoken rule is that each member is responsible only for himself and not what others are doing. Members cannot make assumptions about what is happening in the relationships between the team members and between team member and team leader. The space is for each member to focus on what she needs, her progress and success, but not what the other members need.

CONSISTENCY

In volleyball a foul is called when the server steps on the line while serving the ball. This rule applies regardless of who is playing and when or where the game is being played. Teams need to consistently follow the agreed-upon rules as they set the boundaries and the tone for relationships. Following the rules makes the behavior in the space predictable, which limits uncertainty and increases feelings of safety. Consistent application of the rules helps the team to increase trust as behavior becomes prescriptive and members know more or less what will happen in the room and how they will be treated. People accept the space when the rules are consistently applied and when each team member is treated equally by the other members and the leader.

JUDGMENT

In order for ideas to be generated and exchanged on an ongoing basis in the space, the members must feel they are not being judged. If someone says that an idea is bad, the speaker will shut down and feel embarrassed. In the future, that speaker will hesitate to give ideas, since he feels his ideas may not be good enough for the team. When an idea is praised, the subtle message is that ideas are being compared and other ideas presented were not as good. It means that ideas are unwittingly rated against other, which implies that members are also compared.

Less confident team members may refrain from presenting ideas if they are uncertain of the quality of their ideas. In fact, all ideas are good and members should be encouraged to commit the idea to paper, flesh it out, and determine its feasibility. This conveys that the idea may or may not work and shifts the focus from whether the idea is "good" or "bad."

In the space, members are free to say whatever they want and the leader is not to judge. When my team members mouth off about the organization, I cannot reprimand them. I can explain facts as I know them, or listen and allow the member the freedom to say what she wants.

GOOD INTENTIONS

Not all team members are effective communicators, so it can be difficult for some people to frame and cogently express their thoughts. I assume all team members have good intentions and want a positive outcome. Even though what I am hearing may be contrary to that assumption, I hold on to the thought so that I am able to fully understand what the member is saying before I react.

When listening this way, the leader delays having a reaction and has time to assess the situation before responding. When the leader has emotionally detached from the situation, he can then ask questions to clarify the situation.

If the leader does not agree with or understand the members' behavior, this assumption becomes critical in remaining non-judgmental. Leaders can ask clarifying questions that don't seem judgmental, and help the member feel safe. When the leader assumes the member is operating with negative intentions, then questions become accusations and members begin looking for escape routes.

TEAM NORMING

The rules of the space ensure that members behave in a certain manner that makes the space comfortable. Team members seem to embrace each other, and there is a spirit of togetherness for the team. Do not be fooled by this. This does not mean that your team has normed—that each team member makes decisions that advance the goals of the team. It means that the safe space concept has allowed them to see each other in more neutral light and accept each other's strengths and weaknesses. While the space may act as an accelerator or catalyst for the team to norm, it is not magic. It does not mean that whatever problems existed within the team before have miraculously disappeared.

Your team may act and a sound like a team, but that does not mean that it is a team. Members may be getting along for the leader's sake because they believe this is what the leader wants.

While the safe space contributes to the process of team building, the leader still needs to pay attention and check the team temperature. Regular team meetings and team building sessions should still be conducted. Conversations geared toward checking on the team and how the members feel about the space should continue. The safe space will not exist if members do not participate in the concept. The leader needs to trust that the members want a free space in which to think and create, fail and plan, vent and question. The members need to trust that the leader will not judge or react to the things they say and do in the safe space.

People are generally fearful of new things. There will be members who are unsure of the motives behind the space and look for any loophole to discredit the space and prove that their deepest fears have been realized.

CONCLUSION

The space is inanimate and cannot keep itself safe. We—leaders and members—give the space the power and we need to stand guard for the space. We are the ones to keep it safe. We are the ones to set up the rules, ensure that they are followed, and take members to task when they break the rules.

Keeping the space safe limits the many distractions that prevent team members from implementing their work. Keeping the space safe allows team members to be less emotionally burdened so they can perform at their best. It is about ensuring that the team achieves results.

In the succeeding chapters, we will discuss the things that need to be present from both the team members and the leader to keep the safe space.

8

Trust

Trust is the cornerstone of the safe space concept. Members need to trust that the intention behind the space is for them to win. They need to trust the space to use it, and they need to rely on the leader and each other to keep the space safe.

Trust is an intangible quality that is hard to define. Whom do you trust? Most of us were taught not to trust strangers, not to speak to them, and definitely never get into a car with them. We were also taught to be wary of people who acted, spoke, and looked a certain way. Some of us grew up not trusting the adults who failed, neglected, or abandoned us. There were teachers, caregivers, and others in positions of power who were unkind, derogatory, and at times mean to us and we learned not to trust them. When we become adults, these experiences don't mysteriously disappear; they remain in our memories and flare up when we are put in situations that trigger these memories.

Whenever people talk about their worst work experiences, the word trust and the notion of broken trust come up in different ways. Earlier I talked about the team that didn't trust the finance manager because she selfishly made decisions that would only benefit herself.

Another team was led by Jonathan, an affable leader whose team earned huge bonuses for the large volumes of sales generated every quarter. This was a winning team; yet members were uneasy and tense. A random audit showed that Jonathan routinely inflated sales by booking commission sales as credit sales, which meant that bonuses were grossly overstated. His team members were implicit in his actions, since they suspected the sales figures were inflated but never raised an alarm to senior management.

Team members did not trust Jonathan, even though his intention was aligned with the team's objective—to make more money—because his actions jeopardized the team's credibility. They did not trust each other since they had all accepted the bonuses and were equally implicated as untrustworthy.

With leaders like Jenny, the lack of trust is more subtle. She has favorites and there are rumors that promotions and salary increases are dependent on these personal relationships. Jenny never loses an argument and goes for the jugular whenever possible. She leads and controls her team with fear. Her team members do not trust her.

Derek was a leader who wielded a great deal of power in the company but was not trusted beyond his immediate team. Leaders of other teams often wondered about his agenda when he spoke, and members of other teams referred to him as slimy because of the way he slunk around the office.

There are many examples of leaders who are not trusted because of past actions, the way they treat people, lack of credibility, their decisions, and the way people feel about them. Sometimes the reasons for not trusting them are not related to anything behavioral but may simply come from a gut feeling.

When members say they do not trust enough to share in the space, I assume they're recalling some of these non-trustworthy leaders, which helps me better understand the context of their hesitation. I do not take the statements personally, since they're not about me. Trust is a personal issue, and may reflect past as well as present experiences.

Since trust is essential for keeping the space safe, I engage members in discussions about trust by asking them which people they do trust. Generally, they trust some family members, and people with whom they've been through thick and thin. In my exploration of these relationships in the context of the safe space, I've concluded that there are four levels of trust operating within the space.

The first level of trust is in the process. When a chemist mixes a formula, he relies on a tried and tested chemical equation that gives the intended results. When we are learning something new, we trust what the manual says and proceed, taking one step at a time, facing the challenges as they come, knowing that at the end we will more or less achieve the objective. The team trusts that the rules are the formula to keep the space safe. They trust that the rules will work as intended and each team member will abide by them. The team may be uncertain about the outcome but trust that if the rules are followed, there will be an outcome that everyone can live with. We do not have to understand why things are done the way they are done, or why they work. We just need to do as we said and trust that it works. Trust the intention and work in the space as if you trust it, since actions lead to belief. When we act like we trust the space, we will behave as if we trust the space and reap the benefits of the space, which will prove that it is, indeed, trustworthy.

Initially, team members were fascinated by the idea of being empowered by the safe space concept. This did not mean they trusted me or the space. It meant they could foresee how the space and working with the concept could personally benefit them. They embraced the first level of the trust in the space. The idea was logical and they could understand why and what would make it work. They trusted that if they focused on the work and used the space to get rid of barriers, to plan effectively, they would remove obstacles in their path to winning.

The second level of trust is in the relationship that each person has with the space. Each person has to honor his commitment to the space. Each member is responsible for her own conduct and monitors her relationship with the space. Each member can only be responsible for his personal behavior in the space.

There will be members who do not trust themselves and by extension, they trust no one else. There will be members who lack personal confidence and also have no confidence in the space. These members will determine the extent to which they use the safe space, and the team respects their choice as long as they do not break the rules and they allow others to use the space as they wish. With these members, the leader needs to accept the person's limitations. We are not counselors or psychologists, and cannot assist the members in overcoming personal trust problems. We focus on the work and treat members as we do all others, fairly and consistently. It is up to the member to seek the professional assistance that may make a difference in her outlook. Each member gets out of the space as much as she invests in it.

The third level of trust is that between the people in the room. Each person trusts that the others want the free space as much as she does and will follow the set rules. As team members explore what can be said and done in the room, each one will evaluate others' reactions, especially those of the leader. When there are no repercussions, members will have more discussions and have greater acceptance of the idea. The people who don't trust anyone will limit what they say and do in the space. There will be some individuals who trust only certain team members and will only interact in the space with these people, some who will trust only the leader, and others who will not trust the team leader.

Team members have different relationships with each other. The ones who are friends and are accustomed to collaborating generally have no problem trusting each other. The space serves to formalize their relationships and provide another way to express their relationships. It also offers tangible ways in which they can support each other and acknowledge their relationships.

In my observations, members who hadn't worked together before and had no prior relationship with other team members needed to learn to work and collaborate with each other. These members were given assignments together to build up trust in each other. While this did not always work with members who had different work styles or ethics, it gave each person an appreciation of the other's abilities and shortcomings and helped them to see that trust is separate from work and ability. When members keep discussions confidential and don't repeat what is said in the room, trust is much more likely to develop.

The fourth level of trust is about the leader. The leader is critical to the safety of the space; it is difficult to separate the trust of the space from trust of the leader since the two are indelibly linked. When members do not trust the leader, the space will never be safe. The leader therefore needs to present herself as trustworthy at all times. For the leader to be trusted, she needs to extend trust to the team members to display what trust looks like. Openness in communication, seeking clarification, and asking questions help the leader to be seen as extending trust to the members. The team members will trust the leader when they see her as fair and consistent in the treatment of the team, the distribution of work, and the application of the rules. Members extend personal trust to the leader when the leader doesn't reveal conversations and doesn't disclose personal details. Trust is also built when the leader can separate what is said in the space and not use the details to make assumptions about the member or the member's work.

Trust in my leadership happened in varying degrees; in some cases, it never happened. I don't expect that everyone will trust me; it would be nice, but it doesn't always occur. Members who are wary of me keep me honest. I have to be circumspect and transparent in the way I treat them. I have no problem with lack of trust, because I know it isn't about me. Since the members who did not trust me were in the minority, I did more of the things that made the majority of the team trust me. If my team had had a larger percentage of mistrust, then I would have had to look at myself and review my words and actions in the room. I would also have had to brace myself for some brutal feedback and get ready to apologize and make amends.

Carissa often produced sub-standard work and I started to manage her more closely. Unfortunately, a project meeting was scheduled for a date when I would be out of the country, which meant that Carissa needed to attend the meeting in my stead. I was nervous about her ability but had little choice in the matter since the meeting could not be postponed. I called Carissa to the space and reminded her that she had the intelligence and creativity to excel at the tasks at hand and that she had full autonomy and authority to make decisions related to the project. I assured her that even if she made a mistake we would have many options to fix the errors. This extension of trust made a huge difference in Carissa's performance. Though trust was extended to all team members, I needed to explicitly say to Carissa that I trusted her to improve her performance. She told me later that our conversation gave her the confidence to perform more capably since it clearly demonstrated the trust that I had in her; this implied that she was uncertain of my trust before. Leaders have to reinforce trust with members; we need to reassure them that we trust they will do what is needed and that when problems arise, we will work together to solve them.

Trust has to be earned and it does not happen overnight; it is bolstered by the experiences that the members share in the space. When members have positive experiences in the space, they trust the space more. When they get credit for challenging something, they build more trust in the space. When they hold the space for each other, they create more trust for the space.

Negative feedback can erode the trust in the room depending on the maturity of the receiver and the style of the messenger. Team members who cannot separate themselves from the work or who believe that everything is about them will never trust the feedback they get. When tactless feedback is given, members mistrust the motive for the feedback and lose trust in the space. Trust is not finite and is always held in balance. There will be things said in and out of the room that erode trust and other comments that will build trust. The trick is to keep the conversation about trust going and to keep checking on the level of trust in the room.

TRUST AND NEW MEMBERS

When Sharon joined the team, the current members were nervous. The team had grown accustomed to sharing openly in team meetings and did not trust that Sharon would keep discussions confidential. Each member had a story to tell that implied that though Sharon was well qualified for the job and had a sound work ethic, her behavior was at times undesirable. I trusted that Sharon would see the benefit of having a safe space and want to participate in it. The team shared the safe space rules with Sharon and she agreed to them.

Team members unrealistically and incorrectly assumed that I wanted them to blindly trust anyone who entered the space. Relationships are built over time and are based on shared experiences, so it would be difficult to replicate this with someone new. Just as we don't invite people we've just met into our home, the team shouldn't share intimate details with someone new. The team decided to put Sharon on probation and share only what they were comfortable with in team meetings. As they began to trust her levels of confidentiality, though not necessarily her, they felt comfortable enough to share sensitive issues.

Existing team members often unfairly demand that new members immediately jell with them and may want to coerce new members to immediately embrace the safe space. Just as the team needed time to accept Sharon, she had to come to terms with the safe space. Though she agreed to the rules, she needed time to understand and observe whether people really adhered to the rules and decide if she felt safe in the space as well. New members need time to test and evaluate the space before they can fully embrace it. The new member may choose not to share anything while evaluating the space and this tactic is acceptable. Members need to respect each person's choices

Sometimes members want to dictate and bully others about how the space should be used. Leaders need to remind members that the use of the space is a personal choice and as individuals we are free to choose how and when we use the space.

BROKEN TRUST

When trust is broken it is difficult for members to come into the room. Team members learn to distrust the room because of the experiences they've had with the people in the room—the leader and members.

When the safe space rules are violated, this means that trust is broken. When members disclose what is said in the room to persons outside the team, then people begin to distrust the room and stop sharing in the space. When members stop sharing personal concerns, some level of trust is gone.

Jackie did not understand what it meant to keep conversations confidential even though she had agreed to the rules. Outside the room she would follow up with a member who had disclosed personal details. I explained confidentiality to Jackie and she promised to uphold the rules now that she understood how hurtful her actions had been. Easier said than done, however, and in a month's time, Jackie was at it again. A team discussion was held and Jackie was asked to account for her actions. The team agreed that Jackie was unable to keep conversations confidential, and while they would share work issues with her in the room, she needed to leave the room when they discussed any other confidential matter. The meetings were restructured to accommodate this change and Jackie had to accept the team sanction. The team wanted to maintain the safety of the space and removed the person who jeopardized the space for them.

Sometimes confidence between members is broken outside the safe space. This happens when members do not clearly declare the need for confidentiality outside the physical area deemed the safe space. While some members extend the safe space boundaries beyond the physical room and hold everything said in confidence, some members don't think they should be held accountable for anything said outside that physical room. In these instances, I work with the members to determine what went wrong and to assist them to set boundaries for interactions outside the physical safe space room.

The onus is on the member who's broken confidence to make amends. The member who feels that trust has been broken needs to establish his role in the situation. The member who goes around sharing a story with everyone can accuse no one of breaking confidence because he has chosen to share his story outside the space. These members often don't remember what they said to whom, since the emphasis is on telling the story to as many people as possible to get a desired outcome. Members who love to gossip will always break trust and others need to either invoke the confidentiality rule when talking to them outside the safe space, or limit the information shared with them.

Members also need to be honest with themselves. They know the team gossips, and yet they may tell them confidential information, and then feel upset when the breach happens.

When members regard leadership as untrustworthy, the safe space premise becomes false. When the leader violates trust, he needs to admit he's made a mistake and demonstrate his amends through his behavior, not just what he says, to regain trust. This is not an overnight process; the leader has to prove that he is trustworthy under many different circumstances.

The leader should be heartened by the fact that it is less burdensome for us to trust someone than not to trust them. When we trust, it is easy to listen to what someone is saying and deal with what we hear. It is mentally and emotionally taxing to deal with people whom we do not trust; we second-guess what is being said or try to understand the context of what they mean while at the same time try to say as little as possible to protect ourselves.

OBSERVATIONS

From my observations, I conclude that there is a relationship between employees whose work is superior and the use of the space. Generally, the members whose work is exemplary trust the space. The people who apply themselves and realize they get more power by gleaning the learnings from success and failure are the ones who trust the space. The members who accept personal responsibility and seek personal growth are the ones who trust the space. It is those persons whose work is below par, and those who refuse to make any changes to their personal outlook who often don't trust the space.

The people who trusted the space, took the risks, and ac-- cepted the work challenges are the ones who were promoted out of the team, became subject matter experts in the organization, or became leaders. The ones who trusted in the space and the concept were able to synthesize negative comments, improve their work, and excel. These were the members who trusted the leader would not fail them, or trusted team members would be there to support them. It seems that trust is what allows the members to operate and soar.

The persons who did not trust the space were the ones who were not promoted and seemed to have little personal growth, or developed at a slower rate than the others. They were left behind, remaining in task-focused roles, compared to their team members who migrated to thinking roles. Members who didn't trust the space would not take risks; members who didn't trust the leadership wouldn't learn anything; members who didn't trust peers wouldn't benefit from the feedback and insights of the team.

CONCLUSION

Trust underpins the safe space. Without trust, members will not feel safe in the space, nor will they embrace it. While it is important for the members to trust the space, each member needs to trust himself and trust that other members want the concept to work. It is critical that members trust that the leader will behave more or less in a consistent manner and consistently apply the safe space rules to treat members fairly and equally. The leader needs to extend trust to the members and at times demonstrate that this trust has been extended. The challenge for keeping the space safe rests heavily on the leader's shoulders.

9

Honesty

Honesty is the twin of trust. They work together to keep the space safe. Any situation that involves more than one person can result in at least three versions of the truth—my truth, your truth, and the real truth. When emotions are involved, our reality is distorted and the truth is difficult to "see."

We are familiar with Post-Traumatic Stress Disorder (PTSD), which is a mental or emotional disorder that a victim suffers as a result of a personal experience or after witnessing physical harm or the threat of physical harm. In this extreme situation, the victim has difficulty experiencing the truth of the present reality since his amygdala is dysfunctional. The amygdala is an almond shaped part of the brain that controls fear, anger, and pleasure. It is thought to control flight, fight, or freeze responses so that when faced with perceived or real threats or stressful situations, we run away, attack, or shut down. It also determines what memories are stored and where the memories are stored in the brain.

While PTSD is an extreme reaction of the amygdala, this part of the brain affects each of us on a daily basis. It informs what part of an event we remember and how we react to potentially threatening situations. As a result, it is difficult to always remember the entire truth of a situation.

We have seen staged demonstrations of how the amygdala works on television. A group of people witnesses a startling event such as a mugging and each bystander gives a different version of what happened, including the description of the perpetrator and the sequence of events. All bystanders will agree that the woman was mugged, but each person shares the bit of truth embedded in his or her memory and sometimes that bit of truth has nothing to do with the situation at hand.

This research confirms for me that when more than one person is involved it is possible to have more than one version of the truth. It also suggests that people may not intentionally set out to lie, mislead, or deceive, but sometimes because of how our brain functions it may be impossible for us to know the present reality. By extension, it is impossible for us to know the entire truth. As a result, I approach truth by understanding the event, the desired outcome, and the agenda.

Imagine a quarrel in the office that involves two people and a witness. Each person may have a different version of what happened according to the levels of distress experienced at that time or what past memories were triggered.

When the leader hears about the quarrel, she accepts this as the event—a quarrel happened. How and why it happened and who is at fault are not known at that time. Although the leader may be upset or have other feelings about the event, she needs to get to a neutral state of mind about the event before she does anything. If the team leader decides to follow up on the event, she needs to set a desired outcome for her investigation. For example, she may want to set a standard for handling disputes in the future.

While she may have other desired outcomes such as having members resolve conflict in an effective manner, it's preferable for each conversation to focus on one desired outcome. The desired outcome is best stated as a positive statement that expresses what the leader wants resolved at the end of the conversation. When the leader focuses on the event and on developing a shared, desired outcome for the conversation, it becomes easier to get to the truth.

Each team member may also have desired outcomes—to not get in trouble, to relay the event, or to act as a witness. The leader shares the neutral, desired outcome at the start of the conversation to create an environment that does not trigger the flight or fight response. Since there is no imminent personal threat, team members can piece together the "who, what, and why" of the event.

The desired outcomes will determine the agenda, that is, what each person talks about in the meeting. When all personal agendas are in tandem with one desired outcome, then the versions of the truth are more alike; different desired outcomes mean the truth will more likely be aligned to personal agendas as everyone relates a different story about what transpired.

The assumption that when members agree on a non-threatening outcome, personal agendas will then be aligned may not hold true when emotions have been triggered. The witnesses to that TV mugging all wanted to give a report of the mugging, but sadly very few of them were able to accurately do so.

Consequently, although an atmosphere has been created for telling the truth, it still may not happen. As a result, the focus needs to be on what the team has learned from the event, how it wants to move forward, and the commitment each member can make to limit the chances the event will reoccur. Leaders should stay away from outcomes that include placing blame, since this skews the conversation and may put all members in defensive mode.

MOTIVE

Honesty begins with me as team leader. If I'm being honest, I must clearly communicate my motives to the people around me. It does not matter what the motive is as long as I don't fool myself or others into thinking that it's something else. One way to assess a motive is to ask, "What do I want from this?" If you're not accustomed to stating your needs and wants, you may need to ask, "What do I not want from this?" Equally important is to ask, "Why do I want this?" These answers—pleasing or not—tell others what we want and why at the start of the engagement. Doing so lets the other team members understand our thinking.

Being honest about motives allows others the choice of whether to engage. They can ask questions to clarify their understanding or challenge the motive or help create a new, shared motive. When the motive is unclear, other people may fill in the blanks and make decisions based on false premises. The team member participates based on what she believes and not what the leader wants. The member's ability to choose has been compromised since she has been working with false expectations.

Leaders should always make certain their motives are clear before taking actions that involve team members. When the motives involve saving face, getting even, or are otherwise self-serving, then the leaders need to delay actions until they can come to a motive that is clear of personal reactions.

When I realized that my motive for sanctioning a team member was revenge because she had been speaking critically about me to her peers, I quickly ditched that plan. Leaders should make decisions that focus on work and the team winning when sanctioning team members.

LIES

People lie about personal stuff such as the reason they stayed home, generally because they want sympathy or something else or as an excuse for not getting things done. They also lie to save their skin, such as when they're covering up to buy time or to fix a situation before anyone finds out. They may also lie about the status of a project, saying it's nearly complete when it's not. The motive behind lies is hardly ever about work; it is usually about personal gain.

PERSONAL LIES

Robert, the team leader, gave Sarah several paid days off after her grandmother's death. Over the next two years, tragedy was Sarah's companion as she lost several more relatives and had many funerals to attend. It seemed that she was going through a rough patch but eventually her team learned that her grandmother had not died, which brought into question all the other deaths in her family. "How could she lie?" Robert wondered. He was angry since he'd given her concessions based on those lies, and he thought Sarah had manipulated him simply to get additional time off.

Sarah's lies had nothing to do with Robert; she'd devised a plan that would achieve her desired outcome—additional paid time off. It was not Robert's business to know why she needed time off and he would have been ill advised to make assumptions about her motives. When Robert started giving attributes to both the situation and Sarah, he stopped and reviewed his motives. He admitted his anger, embarrassment, and the need to save face were driving his decision to sanction her. So he decided to remove himself from the equation and think about what the team needed in order to win in the aftermath of Sarah's lies.

Robert did not follow the company's bereavement policy and request a death certificate before he granted the leave. Rather, he became personally involved in Sarah's life and flexed his personal power when he gave her additional time off.

Leaders create their own nightmares when they get personally involved in situations and make decisions outside the organizational policies. When our motive lies outside getting the job done or is serving a personal gain, we become susceptible to these types of mistakes. It's not the leader's responsibility to check whether an employee is lying; this isn't our burden. Our responsibility is to ensure that decision making is not compromised by our personal objectives.

Robert addressed the situation at a team meeting with Sarah

present; he took responsibility for his part in the situation and made amends. He shared the truth without placing any judgment, simply saying that Sarah's grandmother did not die and admitted his culpability in the situation. He stated that he had breached the organization's policy and learned that the rules were also designed to protect leaders; and he announced what he would do differently in the future. He would ask more specific questions, follow company procedure, and ask for evidence when members wanted time off. He asked members to bear with him since his trust was shattered and he needed some time to get back his balance. Robert invited other team members to talk about the experience, encouraging them to use "I" statements and focus on their thoughts and feelings about the issue and ensured that the meeting did not turn into "bash Sarah" time. Robert was surprised to hear that team members were also suspicious about the many deaths in Sarah's family and that they were baffled about the decisions he'd made.

Robert made it clear to his team that lying was unacceptable, but held out that it was a personal choice and members were themselves responsible for the outcomes of their lies. Robert could not force Sarah to make amends to her team; that was something only she could decide.

Robert's options for sanctions against Sarah were dictated by the organization's policies. He reported Sarah's abuse of organizational policy to human resources and Sarah was given a warning letter with a copy placed in her personnel file. Since her work did not suffer as a result of her time off, there was nothing left to discuss.

What if Sarah had admitted to the lies in the safe space?

Robert would still have needed to make amends, take responsibility for his role in the deceit, and report her actions to human resources. It may have made things a little easier for Sarah since her team members would have regarded the confession as making amends in the space. Robert now understands that if Sarah had received no benefits from lying, she would have stopped it long ago.

WORK-RELATED LIES

When the leader stays on top of their work there is little value in the member lying about the status of that work. The leader together with the members set deadlines, monitor, and evaluate the progress of the work. Lies about the status of jobs are used when the leader isn't effective and wouldn't know the difference. Leaders who pay attention are effective at monitoring and evaluating work; those who are diligent at following up on individual projects give members little opportunity to lie. A leader may not be able to check everything that crosses her desk, but short meetings, reports, and constant communication will help to keep members on their toes. If the leader is following up and doing her job, and if there is a safe space for honest discussions, these types of lies rarely occur and when they do they are easily identified and the member is held accountable.

WHITE LIES

White lies and euphemisms are often used to downplay harsh words or to soften the delivery of a message such as saying "passed away" instead of "died." While they may be made with good intentions, such as, not wanting to hurt another's feelings by saying something unkind, they can lead to bigger lies. They can become dangerous when we shy away from delivering the truth or blur the message with niceties so that the original message or intention is lost.

Janice knows that some of her outbursts are inappropriate office behavior. She sheepishly checks with the leader and states that she hopes her behavior wasn't disruptive. The leader doesn't want to deal with the situation and in turn says to Janice, "It wasn't your best behavior." This is a dance, since Janice knows that her behavior was inappropriate and holds out the falsehood. The leader reinforces the falsehood when he uses a euphemism to make Janice feel better or to ignore the situation.

Euphemisms are not easily corrected, since they were collaboratively created. The next time Janice behaves inappropriately, the leader needs to gingerly step around the issue because he has previously co-created with Janice the illusion that while her inappropriate behavior could have been better it was not incorrect. The leader has to either continue ignoring the behavior or now state that it is unacceptable. However, the latter step will show that he's changing his standards, which leaves Janice to either challenge his new description of her behavior or to feel confused or hurt by his change in standards, while the rest of the team watches.

The office is no place for a euphemism, since the team can collaborate to co-create an untruth that will be difficult to undo. It is a lie. It may be a gentle one with good intentions but it is a lie all the same.

CHRONIC LIARS

And then there are the people who lie all the time, about everything, consciously or unconsciously. These persons are to be treated like all others. The leader must not bury his head in the sand. He should confront the member with the team and ensure the team is aware of the lies.

If the person lies about personal issues in the safe space, as long as these lies don't affect anything related to work—performance, absenteeism, company policy—then the leader disregards what is said, as she would for any personal situation discussed by any team member. If the person lies about work, then the leader needs to check for evidence and be extremely cautious in decisions related to this member. The leader also needs to inform the HR department about the problem and where organizational policy mandates the use of counseling sessions, the employee must comply. It is unlikely that a habitual liar will change without psychological intervention. If there is no company policy on handling this type of situation, the team leader must carefully document all instructions and conversations with the member, keeping human resources in the loop about the situation.

DOUBLE STANDARDS

Double standards occur when we treat team members differently under similar circumstances. When Robert gave Sarah time off to attend funerals, he set a precedent and other team members then expected time off to attend funerals. Team members who do not receive time off to attend funerals will think that Robert is unfair in how he treats the other team members.

As leader, I can make one-off concessions to staff for extenuating circumstances and don't have to replicate this policy with all members. Margaret had to leave early for several Fridays to collect her son, since his caretaker was ill. I shared with the team this information and said that other staff could not ask to leave early on Fridays unless there were extenuating circumstances and each request would be examined on its own merit.

FAVORITES

Honesty is violated when leaders have favorites. There is always a team member who appeals to some part of our psyche, maybe because of his personality or how he behaves or something else that appeals to our ego. It is human to like people and to like some people more. People who say yes, who emulate and think like us, or who look a certain way are just easier for us to work with.

Leaders need to be aware of this tendency and admit to themselves when they're drawn to particular individuals. Leaders need to self-monitor to make certain they're not giving more concessions to the members whom they "like." They need to ensure they're willing to honestly say whether they'd make a similar decision if it involved another team member. Members to whom we're not personally attracted will keep a watchful eye on us to see whether we're treating everyone fairly. This is a good thing since they provide a healthy check on our behavior.

DISHONESTY

When teams violate honesty, operate with double standards, play favorites, and tell lies, trust is broken and the team needs time to recover from the breach. This breach is usually worse when the leader is at fault. Team members are usually more generous toward missteps by fellow team members than by the leader. Team members tend to overreact when a leader lies; they take this as an indication of the entire relationship and quickly lose trust.

Few teams have the courage to air these issues, so in the safe space the leader must always check on the levels of honesty in the room. He needs to do this team member by team member since each person has different thresholds for trust. Leaders need to speak the truth—whether it is "I cannot speak about it at this time," or "I have not made up my mind," or even "I do not know." It is better to admit our doubt, anxiety, or lack of information than to pretend we have all the pieces.

If the issues are particularly sensitive and the leader is not at liberty to speak, he should say so. When the CEO shared his decision about a leadership change for the new division, it was understood that this was confidential. I told the team members that while I knew who it was, I was not in a position to disclose the information and they respected that.

CONCLUSION

In the safe space, members can choose to unload anything they wish. If they come into the space and fabricate a story, it should not matter to the leader. The space is for their use; if they choose to lie about what they need, it is not the leader's job to call them out. The space is one of no judgment, so therefore members can speak as they want. The listener is not supposed to hold on to what they are saying, make decisions based on the discussion, or follow up. When the listener adheres to the rules, it does not matter if the talker lies. Each person is responsible for how she deals with her own honesty. The leader's role in the room is to be present and attentive, and to support the members by allowing them to take risks.

Challenge the Team

was part of an interview panel where the candidates were all intelligent and confident young people under age twenty-five. They had college degrees, and were working toward another advanced degree such as an MBA or MA. These were not book-worms; they were sociable and assertive creatures. One was a costar of a local talent television program, and another did marketing on weekends. They were hoping to get a new position with better prospects for the future. I was humbled. I could have hired any of them and been happy. They were all young, intelligent, qualified, and hungry for experience. They were inexperienced but communicated how eager they were to learn.

As I walked back to my office, I looked at the team members. They were older, some less qualified, held long-standing posts, and were secure in their jobs. They did their jobs according to the description of their positions and collected an annual bonus. They seemed unaware of the realities of the job market and the competition that they faced.

The more I thought about it the madder I got. What were we doing? Why did team members have a sense of entitlement? Was this good enough for the organization?

My team members are good workers. They show up every day, get their tasks done without complaining, take their breaks, and are punctual. They take their sick leave and paid vacations and they work. They meet their targets and get a bonus. Yet there are no promotions for them, because they do not make a difference. Their work is appreciated, but they are drones. Any other warm body could replace one of them.

BRING YOURSELF

I challenge team members to bring themselves to the office. These men and women plan events, have hobbies, solve problems, are responsible for others, and make decisions on a daily basis; yet when they walk through the company's door, they collectively morph into a being that thinks and reacts the same way. The office becomes a bubble in which drones wait for the end of the day to be released back to their real lives. Just look around your office. What would it be like if these decision makers and creative thinkers were part of your team? What would it be like if your team members could bring these parts of themselves to the office? We were never explicitly told not to bring ourselves to the office, but we were never explicitly told that we could. We learned that we needed to behave in a professional manner at the office, which meant that we had to adopt another persona and not be our casual selves. However, leaders can contradict this belief and encourage members to invite all of themselves to the office. People need permission to integrate their lives, their creativity, and their intelligence into the professional demeanor they have at the office.

BRING A PROJECT

I want to work with people who make a difference. I do not need team members to be the best or the brightest, but I do need them to see what can be done for the team, department, or company and bring in ideas about how to do it. I need them to start something, to say something, to do something that makes them better, the team better, the company better, and by extension, me better. I want to work with people who are not afraid to fail and will bring forth ideas and projects.

There are corporations that have an environment that encourages employees to work on their own or in a team on their own projects, using ideas they have brought forth. Sometimes employees are given additional resources to develop these projects. The more ideas, the more innovation, the more the company wins. The difference between these organizations and mine is that these companies have actively created environments for creativity and for projects to happen. As leaders we can mimic this with our team members, even if the rest of the organization does not have such a system in place. We have the authority to give our team members permission to be their most creative and intelligent by encouraging them to generate a project. Unless we

LEAD YOUR TEAM TO WIN

do this, team members are never going to bring forth any ideas. Leaders have a one-dimensional view of the organization, and can only generate ideas from this perspective. Members have a different view of the organization and offer unique ideas.

Team members were uncertain. They said things like, "We don't have the authority to present a project." And, "Are you giving us more responsibility?"

I had to literally give them permission to bring in a project before they could engage in the conversation. "Think of something you want to see done, or a problem that needs to be solved, and let's see how we can get do it," I responded. "It may not be for our team, but we can offer up the idea and work with other people to get it done." Team members didn't immediately furnish new ideas. They were afraid they'd be judged or rejected, and they didn't want to look dumb. In fact, the ideas were a mix of tried and true, and others were distinctive.

As leaders we provide the framework and tools for members to flesh out ideas. Initially, I spent considerable time asking members open-ended questions to help them develop their ideas and determine how to implement them. Documentation helped the team to conceptualize ideas and develop how much time and money would be required to bring an idea to fruition.

The learning curve was steep and I needed to be patient as members went through the process. Now team members work together to vet each other's ideas and complete documentation before bringing them to me. No ideas are stolen and no one takes credit for another's work; there are no secret projects and the owners pitch ideas they're interested in. Members get credit for ideas that are converted to projects while the ideas that don't come to fruition aren't counted.

Team members grow more comfortable sharing, since they are fully supported by peers and benefit from the questions members ask and the room given for them to think. The more that members support each other the less work there is for me. All ideas, whether or not they come to fruition, make the team look good and get us noticed by executives. The CEO notices that this team is coming up with ideas, working out details, and saying what needs to happen. These ideas are not written on a napkin; they are documented proposals, with the risks duly noted and the cost-benefit analysis done. The team leader looks great and the members look great.

PERMISSION TO FAIL

When the leader invites the team to bring ideas, she is giving team members the opportunity and permission to fail. At every step of the idea generation and project execution, members can fail. Leaders need to let members know it's acceptable to fail and that failure is an element of success.

If a new idea does not pass the feasibility test, then the member is freed up to start thinking about a new idea while getting rid of the old one. If the project is in execution and something goes awry, the team needs to fix the problem, learn from it, and move on. The leader needs to help the team understand that failure is a potential outcome of risk taking and trying something new. Failure is mitigated by making plans and thinking through the project. It is not something to fear. We all fall; what makes the difference is how quickly we get up and go again. My team members know that when the idea is a success, they gain the fame of being the generator of the idea. And when the idea fails, they are guaranteed anonymity.

PERMISSION IS NOT APPROVAL

Permission to bring an idea does not equate to acceptance. I offered to set up a coaching program for newly hired managers but my CEO refused. Even with the "best" of ideas, it is the leader's prerogative to say no. Everyone in the organization is privy to different information and opinions. The CEO said no based on his view of the organization and the people I wanted to coach.

Leaders know what is happening or about to happen in the organization and can usually see that an idea may be brilliant but still won't work at that particular company. Only we can determine if the risk, when weighed against all the other priorities, is worth it. We all have someone we need to impress so there is no value in pitching a mediocre idea upward. Just as my CEO rejected my coaching idea, so too can I reject the team's ideas.

Great ideas also die political deaths. Team members know that my motive is to win and that we operate within a larger organization filled with internal politics and machinations. For an idea to find support, the timing must be right and the people who can support it must be aligned to the cause. Team members may be miffed that their idea was not accepted, but this should not affect team morale. Not getting approval shouldn't kill enthusiasm and creativity and members shouldn't feel betrayed. They will still bring ideas.

When I can give the reason for not advancing a project, I do; when the reasons are sensitive and I cannot share them, I remind members that my motive is to win. As innovative as an idea may be, if it does not allow us to win it won't be adopted. Team members may not agree with me, but as with everything else, the buck stops with me.

A year later, my CEO agreed that I could coach some of the junior managers. Ideas do not have to be immediately implemented; sometimes you have to wait for better conditions before the idea can work. While you're waiting, you can plan and wait for the opportune moment for execution.

I sign off on all ideas that are accepted, regardless of the implementation date, to show my commitment to seeing them come to fruition. The team members who generated the ideas also sign the document so they share ownership and recognition.

I will not sign a document that concerns me; I will work with the member to eliminate the areas of concern before I sign off. If there remain doubts or unanswered questions the proposal is rejected. Once I have signed the document, I will not refute the proposal when the CEO questions the validity of the project. I will return the document to the team member if the CEO wants additional data or questions answered, so that the member retains responsibility for the work.

CHALLENGE THE WORK

The leader needs to hold high standards for all work and not accept substandard work. When members are accustomed to delivering mediocre work, it is difficult to break this pattern, which will not serve the leader or the purpose of the space. Leaders should not accept or fix mediocre work. No one likes the idea of reworking a proposal, but if members do not get it right the first time, they have to do it again. This is the way we learn to do better. When we are learning to play an instrument, or try a new dance, we make mistakes; but we keep trying again and again until we get it right.

ASK 'HOW' AND 'WHAT' QUESTIONS

I am a Certified Professional Facilitator and Certified Evidence-based Coach. The training from both professions has instilled in me the importance of open-ended questions. They challenge the responder to think and ensure that the questioner does not impose her ideas on the responder. It takes effort to use this approach. The questioner has to consciously decide to do so.

Here are some definitions so you can see the difference in how you ask questions:

Closed-ended questions are what lawyers call leading questions and require a yes or no answer. They are what we see on legal television shows when the lawyer asks the witness to answer the question only with a "yes" or "no." The answer is implied in the questions. While this approach may work for lawyers, it won't work with our team members. Consider these questions starting with a verb such as "Were you in the kitchen?" or "Did you paint your nails?" or "Is it raining?" All these questions have a 50/50 chance that the answer is either yes or no and if the person cannot answer or doesn't want to tell a lie, then the answer becomes maybe. These questions are leading the person to a yes or no outcome. They do not require further information and they are really about the asker. The asker has predetermined some answers and wants to prove that one of his assumptions is correct. For example, if someone asks, "Is it raining?" that asker wants to decide whether to carry an umbrella.

By asking someone if she painted her nails, the asker has clearly looked at the nails and made her own conclusion, but wants to be absolutely certain. If Mom asks whether you washed the dishes, it's because she wants to ensure that the dishes are washed.

Most times the answer to this type of question is followed by a "but." The responder doesn't want to lie if the answer is not 100 percent yes or 100 percent no, so saying "but" provides some wiggle room.

Responders are not enthusiastic about these questions and don't offer more information. Since the questioner cannot think of all the scenarios that may need a yes or no answer, some scenarios are missed. When the questioner asked, "Why didn't you tell me?" the answer will always be, "You never asked." Closed-ended questions leave the questioner with the responsibility to guess what has happened and follow up with the right question.

Open-ended questions show that the asker doesn't know the answers. Using them might suggest the questioner isn't the smartest person in the room and doesn't know everything. This is a hard pill for some leaders to swallow but it's the truth. We will not know unless we ask. Open-ended questions begin with "how" or "what." I tend to exclude "why" questions since the answer begins with "because" and the responder is often immediately on the defensive.

"What" and "How" questions: Sometimes the questioner inserts an assumption into the question that reveals her conclusions. Consider: "What did you paint on your nails?" The questioner has made the decision that the nails were painted. A better question would be, "What did you do to your nails?" It takes practice to work on these questions. In the interim, leaders should refrain from asking questions and instead invite information from members. For example, "Tell me about your nails." This opens up the conversation to go in any direction the responder wants to take it.

Leaders can help members improve their work by helping them focus on the objectives they are trying to achieve and by asking questions such as: What is the purpose of this? Who is our audience? What is the desired outcome? How are you going to achieve it? It is also more difficult to ask members the right questions and watch them struggle as they search for the answer. You can't answer for them, as that doesn't help the member understand the work. While this can take more time on the leader's part, it will pay off in the long run as members learn the types of questions they need to ask themselves as they retain responsibility for the work. Rework provides opportunity for on-the-job training. When the leader takes over, corrects, and finalizes the work, members are deprived of the chance to grow, develop their own style, bring efforts to completion, and take full responsibility for their work.

It is the impatient leader who fixes the work since he knows what to do. The member will learn nothing and will continue to bring in work for the leader to fix. Both leader and member will be stuck in this routine until the leader helps the member learn how and what to do to improve her work.

Leaders need to focus on their own work instead of fixing members' efforts. The separation of duties helps leaders maintain an overview of the team's work, so they're not mired in the daily activities. Leaders need to maintain a strategic focus on the team and its role in the organization.

Leaders often use pending deadlines to justify the fact that they're doing the work. However, they really need to set realistic deadlines that reflect where the member is on the learning curve. A member whose work is up to scratch can have a tighter deadline than someone who has less experience. Leaders also need to factor in rework time in establishing deadlines.

When team members correct work, leaders should compliment them for taking into account the feedback and working to produce a better quality outcome. Members feel better when they hear they did a good job; it helps them forget the pain of going through the steps over and over again. It's like the ballerina who gets flowers at the end of the show. She forgets about the many hours of practice and the teacher shouting at her as the glory surpasses the pain.

THE PARETO PRINCIPLE

This concept, created by Joseph M. Juran, says that 80 percent of effects come from 20 percent of the causes, or that 20 percent of the defects cause 80 percent of the problems. As applied to project management, this means that 20 percent of the work consumes 80 percent of the time and resources. As applied to management, it is recommended that 80 percent of a leader's time should be spent managing, leading, and planning, with 20 percent on doing the actual work. I take a similar approach when approving work in the office. I establish some non-negotiables based on what is practical and required for the execution of the work. For example, the calculations must be accurate, the spelling perfect, and the deadline met. I accept work that meets the purpose and stated objectives; I don't accept work that is fundamentally incorrect. If 80 percent of the report is comprehensible, I ignore the 20 percent that, on analysis, reflects that the writing style is not like mine. I focus on the accuracy of the data therein and not the way the sentences are constructed.

My work is not perfect, nor do I want it to be perfect. I extend the same courtesy to team members. Once it is 80 percent or higher, I accept the work and we move on to something else.

LET THE TEAM SET STANDARDS

The team sets its standards for reports and the completion of work. These are simple statements: all work must conform to the same standards so it becomes obvious when work comes in below those standards. We also have standards for the way work is done. We ask for help at least five days before the deadline. This enables members to understand how to get work done and puts some structure into the way we work.

We also evaluate the work of each other against the standards, and give feedback in a set manner. When Marianne gave a presentation, we all gave feedback in the agreed manner. We start with the good—praising and congratulating what's positive. Then members say what they heard and explain why it did or didn't work for them. We then ask the presenter specific questions so we can understand the choices that were made, and then we stop. The presenter then summarizes what she heard, asks any clarifying questions, and then states what she learned and what changes she will make. Feedback is for the presenter, not the observer. Marianne didn't need to be told what to do; she listened to the experiences of the team members and was able to conclude on her own what she needed to improve from their comments.

CONCLUSION

Leaders need to challenge members to present a high-quality standard of work and take risks so that they will grow. The safe space offers the safety net that provides a comfortable landing in times of failure. Members will accept and work on larger-scale projects and accept more responsibility as they experience success. Leaders need to get out of members' ways and support them from the sideline, giving them the praise they deserve when they succeed and the commiseration they need when they fail.

Decision Making

The safe space is violated when leaders fail to lead. If you want a great team, then you need to be a great leader. This does not mean you have to change your personal beliefs, alter your personality, become a touchy–feely person, or lose your sense of wit. It means you need to develop a style that makes you an effective and great leader.

I am sarcastic and may not be the most approachable person, but team members never doubt my honesty, fairness, consistency, and ability to lead them. I am constant in both my personality and my responsibility to the team members. I can't change my personality since I'm not interested in putting forth the effort to do so. I also don't want to pretend to be someone I'm not, since then I would be operating under false pretenses. I leave my personality alone and instead focus on my leadership skills.

While I will engage team members in decision making, at the end of the day I'm ultimately responsible for everything that emanates from my team. The team celebrates my leadership in its successes and tells me where I need to support its failures. I accept both admonition and praise as the barometer of my performance. My team members know that I share in their wins and their failures as well.

CHANGING MY MIND

Leadership for me is about decision making, and I sincerely believe there are no right or wrong decisions. I am not a surgeon and don't handle life or death matters, and under most circumstances, if I change my mind, it doesn't cost anyone anything. I once read that Warren Buffett attributed his success not to knowing when to buy stock but rather knowing when to sell it. He would change his mind about the quality of a stock, even when his peers disagreed, and he would sell the stock just before it began to dip in value. In this way he minimized his losses and held on to his shirt when others lost theirs.

Decisions are vehicles to take us to where we want to go. Changing the route may save gas or avoid difficult terrain; in the end we will arrive at our destination. I am not vested in the actual decision but I am vested in the outcome. This frees me to immediately change any decision I've made and not lose face. I can misinterpret data or be proven wrong; I can see someone else's point of view and, based on this new information, change my mind.

Changes are not done on a whim. For me, decision making is like building a puzzle. As I become clearer about the picture I'm building, I can easily shift around pieces to create it. The more pieces of the puzzle I solve, the more I know where the other pieces fit. I will not change my mind about building the puzzle as I am committed to that decision; but as I get more information, I may need to revise an earlier decision about how the pieces fit in order for the puzzle to be completed correctly.

The best thing about a bad decision is that you can abort it and make a new one. Even if you have spent $5 million and then realized the decision is wrong, it's better to stop and come to a new conclusion. There are consequences and you could lose your job, but what is the alternative? Would you spend $100 million trying to make the wrong things right? That would surely end your career.

The leader's worst enemy is her ego. We don't ever want to look like we don't know what we're doing. Ego tells us to hide our faults, to pretend the decision is right, to pray for a different outcome, and that if we push hard enough, we can miraculously make the wrong right. Ego very rarely tells the truth. Ego wants to be right at all costs. The worst thing about being wrong is trying to make a wrong right, which is like the alchemist's gold. It just isn't going to happen.

LET OTHERS TAKE THE LEAD

Leaders do not always have to be at the helm of the troops; we can effectively lead from behind. While this would seem to contradict the very meaning of the word lead, it allows members to learn how to make decisions and make mistakes in a safe environment.

Shelly planned an emergency drill for the organization and decided to omit some teams from the drill. She asked my opinion and I indicated that the results wouldn't be valid if a portion of the population was omitted. She disagreed and ran the drill with the exclusions. After analyzing the drill results she popped into my office and said, "You were right." Even though I determined what the drill outcome would be, I had to get out of Shelly's way. She needed to run with her decision, get her own results, and make her own conclusions. The incorrect decision did not cost any money, and what she learned was priceless. Shelly could take full leadership responsibility for the drill since whatever the outcome, the predetermined organizational risk was minimal.

Team members need to practice making decisions so they'll get better at making them and gain more confidence in doing so. While all decisions have a cost impact, the outcomes that are not critical to the organization's bottom line provide good training ground for decision making.

The leader can determine what decisions team members can make by weighing the consequences of an incorrect decision. If the fallout is immaterial, then the member can freely make decisions and deal with the consequences. There are many decisions that team members can make on a daily basis. What training program to attend? What project to work on? Who are the project team members? How will a project be completed?

DELEGATION

In task delegation, the leader makes a decision and gives the member responsibility for enacting the actions related to the desired outcome. True delegation allows members to make decisions and be responsible for all consequences. This frees team members to be independent of the leader and develop decision-making skills. In the long run the leader becomes less involved in operational decisions and consequently can be more strategic on a daily basis. When the reins of responsibility are handed over, leaders need to walk away while still keeping a watchful eye. Think of a child learning to ride a bike. Someone more experienced holds the back of the bike and lets it go when the child is steady on the wheels. Some kids panic and tumble while others keep on riding when they realize that no one is holding the bike. Eventually even those who tumble get back on the bike with the knowledge that they can in fact ride.

Team members will at first timidly make decisions and will get bolder after they've had success. Leaders need to create an environment that encourages risk taking and give members the tools to support success.

RESPONSIBILITY

I have been called out in meetings when the data supplied was erroneous because I didn't read the entire report. I've been asked to explain things that I had no idea were in the report. While I silently kick myself under the table and restrain from throttling the team member, I know that it's really my fault. I've seen leaders distance themselves from these types of situations and place the blame solely on the members. For me, such behavior is unacceptable.

When team members do something wrong, it doesn't help

to blame. Assigning blame shifts the focus from the mistake to the person. Blame comes with its ugly twin, shame. When someone feels shame, he feels less of a person, starts to compare himself negatively to others, and is discouraged from taking future chances. While I promote a "no blame policy," I believe that the person who's wrong needs to take responsibility, admit he made a mistake, and make amends.

When Stanley tried to contract his cousin's catering firm, Eat Well, to provide lunches for the strategic meeting, I understood that his intentions were to save the company money and provide his cousin's start-up with a client. While these intentions could not be faulted, the execution of the intention violated company policy. He made a mistake; yet though he was culpable, I didn't blame him. He needed to walk his cousin through the vendor application process and ensure that the company certified Eat Well as a vendor before an order could be placed.

Team members have to take responsibility and follow up appropriately and professionally when they do something incorrectly. If the report is incorrect and doesn't make sense, then they, not the team leader, need to fix it. If they've offended someone with their behavior, they need to diffuse the situation; the team leader should not step in.

WHEN THINGS GO WELL

When times are good, give your team members lavish praise. People do even better when they know they're doing well. How many times have you done something you thought was executed well and no one gave you feedback? Did you want to do it again?

The teachers for whom we tried hardest were the ones who praised our efforts and championed our ambitions. They saw in us what we couldn't see in ourselves, and we pushed ourselves to move closer to the dream they held for us.

The leading customer service companies spend their energies focusing on the things they do well and ensuring that customers experience more of these good things, more often. By extension, team members will engage in the habits the leader fosters, especially if they understand that these habits will bring them success. Leaders therefore need to highlight what team members are doing well so that members will replicate the efforts.

I have never met anyone who disliked being complimented and praised. Even those who are uncomfortable with the attention or unaccustomed to praise will be pleased with receiving kudos. Team members will not get big heads but they may develop greater confidence. They will not become arrogant but they will be more assertive. Leaders should not be afraid to treat team members well, or praise them when they do something of note. This creates a positive cycle of right action, praise, more right action, more confidence, more assertiveness, and more right action—more often.

Organizations tend to focus on the leaders, and praise them when the team members do well. When that happens, leaders need to redirect the praise to the team members. When I receive emails praising the success of an initiative, I respond and copy the member involved. I take every opportunity to publicly appreciate and praise the work of the team members involved by saying something like, "We all have Allison to thank for the outcome."

Members want to be recognized by their peers and other

leaders for their successes. Monetary benefits related to the success should also be shared. The leader can negotiate on behalf of the members, regardless of the company's policy. If the organization does not pay bonuses to members then the team leader should find creative ways to share the benefits of success with the members involved.

WHEN THINGS GO WRONG

So many things can go wrong including missed deadlines, errors, and unspoken expectations that haven't been met. In these situations, my emotions include anger that something has gone wrong, annoyance with myself for not spotting an error, not paying attention, or not asking the right question, and fear that the error may make me look dumb because it was simple.

Rationally, I know that an error is not the end of the world and though there may not be a fix, there will be another day to make amends. Therefore, during this emotional state I take no action. I'm aware that these are just feelings and this isn't the time to make decisions, but instead a time to retreat and plan. When the feelings subside, I can objectively examine the situation.

This is a big test for the leader. Our natural instinct is to save ourselves and remove ourselves from danger. It is healthy to want to throw the member under the bus and extricate ourselves from the situation. But we cannot do this, as it will erode any trust that members have in the leader.

When something goes wrong, I am still the team leader; I need to lead people out of the mess and make them believe it is still acceptable to take risks in the future. The safe space is violated when leaders don't accept responsibility for team failures and don't help members learn from the mistakes that were made. Sharing successes gives me the authority to share the failures as well. In the public's eye, I do not pass on the failure to the team member. As leader, I accept the fallout as a reflection that I am not being effective. In private, I work with the member to ensure she understands the problem and how and why it occurred. She needs to make amends for the error and is responsible for any corrective action that is agreed on. She knows that while the buck stops with me, the responsibility for cleaning up the mess is hers.

MISTAKES

Mistakes occur when decisions are made with limited or incorrect information and provide rich opportunities for learning and growth. Most mistakes can be fixed; they are not the end of the world. But when a mistake is made, we put intense heat on it and watch as the resulting furor leaves behind festering pools of low self-esteem and relationships in need of mending. Usually when team members make a mistake, I catch it because I have paid attention, read the report, or asked the right questions.

Sandy used my company-issued credit card to sign up for some $7 online courses. Ten minutes later, she asked for my address and then for my date of birth. I asked, "What does that have to do with paying for the course?"

She answered, "I have to set up a PayPal account to pay for the program."

"What does finance think about setting up a PayPal Account?" I asked.

"I did not ask finance," she said. When she checked with the finance department, she was told that PayPal accounts are not to be set up with company credit cards. If I hadn't asked the right questions and not been sensitive to the one about my age, the team member would have set up a PayPal account and violated the accounting code. I prevented the mistake because I paid attention.

LESSONS LEARNED

The lessons learned are important in order to replicate success and to limit the repetition of failure. Depending on the size and impact of the big project, the lessons will be formally documented or there will at least be a conversation. We examine what happened, why it happened, and how it can be repeated or prevented. The focus is on learning from mistakes and continuing the right behavior to ensure success. I use the same learning approach in both outcomes so the member can associate the feelings that she has, the things that were done, and the results that were gleaned. Team members are asked:

What made it a success or failure?

What did you do differently from other times?

How do you feel about the success/failure?

What did you learn?

How will you carry the learning forward to other jobs?

What will you do differently in the future?

In times of failure, add the question: What are you going to do about it?

This helps the team members make an indelible link between what they're feeling, what they did, and the success or failure of the project. Linking the outcomes to the feelings makes it personal, and when members determine what brought them success or failure, they can do more or less of it. Focusing on the next steps in cases of failure helps to reinforce the message that the failure is a learning opportunity and that corrective action is needed.

CONCLUSION

Most of us were not born leaders. We read books, attended courses, and developed a style that worked for us. And we honed it over the years. We made mistakes along with horrible decisions, and learned from them. Our team members are just like us and therefore can learn to lead and make decisions. We can create a team in which the members make great decisions every day and effectively execute the decisions.

This is how a winning team works. The leader of such a team does not have to spend time micromanaging and directing people's work. With this type of team, the leader can get real support for completing projects. This is a winning team with a winning leader. In this type of team everyone wins.

Issues Are the Problems

Problems occur all the time. Plans go awry, something unexpected pops up and our resources, time, and energies are spent righting the wrong, trying to get back on track to achieve our objectives. Sometimes we get lucky and the problems have been anticipated in our risk analysis so that we can easily execute our mitigation plans and get back on track. Sometimes the situation is totally unexpected when the variables have changed and we have no control over events and cannot mitigate against them.

These are genuine problems and challenges that pop up from time to time. These are different from regularly recurring problems in our organizations and teams that just will not go away. Very often we experience these recurrent problems as cause and effect (whenever it rains he's late) or an act that recurs regardless of the circumstances (he is always late).

These recurrent problems are patterns. In the past a certain response was given to a stimuli or situation, and now whenever that stimulus is assumed to be present, the response is the same. It may also be the result of an underlying behavior that is unseen— every morning he runs for thirty minutes before he goes to work. He wakes up late, and then he runs for thirty minutes so he gets to work late.

The individual who is displaying the behavior may be unaware of the cause and effect of the situation and may not even remember when and what occurred for the pattern to be set. He may not experience it as a problem; he may think it's something he's always done, should do, or must do. There's no thought about it; the response is automatic. He runs every morning to be in a good mood and to get pumped for the day ahead. He doesn't correlate being late to the good feeling.

Organizations are comprised of people and therefore patterns will show up in the culture of the organization, in the way that people behave and treat each other.

ORGANIZATIONAL PATTERNS

Simon was a young accountant who dressed in expensive clothing and had a lifestyle that far exceeded that of his peers. He and his family were doing well and were involved in real estate ventures. A random query revealed that Simon had defrauded the company of millions of dollars over a three-year period. In his extravagant scheme, he set up a series of dummy companies, wrote bogus contracts in the company's name, and forged check payments. Simon was a problem, but he was not the only one. Two years before, under the same leader, Marcia had misappropriated funds to set up a bed and breakfast. She employed the same methods of fake contracts and forged checks to purchase the property. She, like Simon, was fired for fraud.

While Marcia and Simon were both opportunistic people with dubious values, they illustrate the fact that the company created the conditions for the pattern of fraud. The methods that the two used to defraud the company were the same, and in their defense statements, they suggested that other people were enacting similar fraudulent transactions. While the company got rid of the problem by terminating the pair, the issues remained. The control procedures at the company were ineffective and, as a result, the purchase to pay system was easily compromised. When the organization revamped its purchase to pay system and established new policies and procedures, there was no longer a problem with fraud. But until the organization dealt with the issue of ineffective controls, the pattern of fraud continued.

INDIVIDUAL PATTERNS

Problems usually reflect something that has occurred repeatedly, and until this pattern is broken, the difficulties will continue. Chances are the team member who has a problem with deadlines has always had a problem with deadlines. It's the same with our personal lives. If we're broke, chances are we've always been broke, expected to be broke, or were raised broke. Nothing happens overnight. Patterns are formed from the way we grew up, the things we were told, what we believe, and our personal experiences. These habits become ingrained in us and very often we are unaware that the pattern exists.

Germain was a popular young man with a beautiful smile and a personality to match. His work was excellent but was always delivered late. Germain argued that his tardy delivery reflected his high quality performance that required a lot of effort to produce. Even with extended deadlines, the problem continued; Germain was stuck in a pattern of being late with his work.

I asked Germain to keep a detailed schedule of the use of his time—the time he arrived to and left work, bathroom breaks, telephone calls, actual working hours, and any other use of time. He agreed and we scheduled a meeting to review the results.

When we met and analyzed the spreadsheet he became very quiet. The schedule clearly showed there was an imbalance between the time that Germain actively spent on his tasks and his down time. He could now understand that not meeting deadlines was a result of a bigger issue about how he used his time.

A huge chunk of his time was spent chatting with his peers on the phone and in person as they sought advice from him about their personal and professional lives. While Germain clearly was an informal leader and had won the trust of his peers, his helping nature was now a hindrance to his performance. When Germain answered the "how" and "what" questions about his use of time, he divulged that he felt he had to live up to people's requests for his time. He felt badly about saying no or that he was too busy, and he felt obliged to stop his work and provide them comfort.

When asked how he felt about it, he was annoyed and embarrassed. He realized that he was not the high performing professional he thought he was. He liked his job and it was important to him, but his behavior didn't reflect that. He also felt sad and disappointed that his peers were insensitive to his needs for working hours.

Germain decided he would hold court with his friends during his lunch hour. He would encourage them to make their visits to his desk less frequently and he would learn to say, "Let me call you back. I'm busy right now." A pattern of not meeting deadlines revealed that Germain's real issue was an inability to set boundaries around the use of his time with his peers. He made himself available whenever they needed to talk to him and as a result they bombarded him whenever they wanted. If we had focused only on the problem of his work being late, we would not have gotten to the core of the issue and his tardy delivery would have never stopped.

UNEARTHING THE ISSUE

The leader's task is to distinguish between a pattern and a true problem. Once the pattern has been identified, the leader needs to assist the member so he can see and understand the pattern and how it affects the situation at hand. The leader also needs to work with the member to determine what the true issue is so that the pattern can be addressed and eventually stopped.

The first step is for the manager to observe whether there is a pattern. Whenever someone does the same action over and over and cannot link consequences to the action, he may be operating in a pattern.

Whenever the member cannot correlate the cause and effect but thinks this is just the way it happens, then he may be operating in a pattern. Germain was unaware that his lateness was a problem so he simply saw it as an outcome of being a perfectionist with his work.

After the observation, the leader needs to collect third-party evidence to objectively inform the member about the behavior. If possible, the evidence should be collected by the team member to remove any doubts about the veracity of the data. Germain's timetable provided an independent record of how he spent his time, and it removed my feelings, observations, and assumptions from the conversation. The focus was on what the schedule revealed about Germain's use of time.

In situations where it's difficult to collect evidence, observations from other team members can be used since members often have more faith in observations from peers than those of the leader. A survey provides an easy way to collate data and provide feedback while protecting the individual opinions of the team. After the data has been collated, the leader needs to bring it to the team member's attention. The member needs to interpret and make deductions from the evidence provided. The member is not required to explain the reasons behind what the evidence displays; he needs to interpret what the data means. Germain was able to explain that he did not work as many hours as he previously thought.

The empirical evidence and the conclusions drawn from the evidence are both necessary precursors for awareness. Once the member interprets and understands the evidence, he can become aware of what it means.

It is only when the team member is aware of the problem and has identified the reasons behind the issue that he can possibly understand the difficulty. Germain became aware when he realized his work was late because he wasn't setting boundaries for his peers and not because he was a perfectionist.

The following series of "what" and "how" questions helped Germain recognize his issues and get to the root cause of his problem. Some of the questions were:

What does the schedule show?

How do you feel about it?

What does it tell you?

What makes the evidence appear that way?

How would you prefer the evidence to look?

What do you have to do for it to look the way you want?

What did you learn?

What are you going to do differently?

What three things can you do to get the evidence the way you want?

This line of questioning helps the member make the link between current and desired behavior, and leads him to uncover what he needs to do to get that desired outcome. Very often people are not aware of behavioral problems since we're accustomed to operating in patterns and we don't link events to behaviors. Germain was being a good peer when he listened to the problems of others. With awareness he had a new way of looking at things and he could discern what was wrong. While the issues and people are intermingled, the leader needs to find the issue in each situation and deal with that.

MONITORING THE PATTERN

Once the team member is aware of the problem and its root cause has been identified, it is important to determine how the behavior can be changed. The focus should be on doing things differently. When Germain's peers stop at his desk, he needs to remind himself about why he's unable to meet deadlines and replace his usual behavior with a request to postpone the conversation.

It's difficult to change a habit. We need to replace the existing behavior with a new one. The more our actions reflect the new habit, the less we do it the old way. While forming the new habit we need to have a barometer of the old. Germain's deadlines were a good way to gauge what was happening. When he missed a deadline, it was an indication that he needed to look at his use of time and see where he had fallen short. He would quickly recalibrate the use of his time.

ACCOUNTABILITY

Though the issue may be related to a pattern, the team member remains accountable for the consequences of the action. The leader cannot give the member a pass because the issue has been unearthed. The leader works with the member to monitor the problem, but the member is ultimately responsible for any consequences. The leader remains focused on the issues and the consequences and does not engage in blaming the individual. The member is now sharply aware of what happened and understands why the pattern has developed. He can link the consequences to the issue. It's now up to the member to address the issue and limit its negative effects. Now Germaine has no excuse for his late delivery. When he's late, I can ask, "How is your timekeeping?" and give him room to self-examine and self-correct. Tardiness means he is not managing his time well and cannot give any excuses, since both he and I understand the truth behind his late delivery. Since he already knows he's failed to manage his time efficiently, there's no need to berate him.

CONCLUSION

Patterns are formed over a long period of time, and people are not able to immediately change them. However, becoming aware of the pattern is the first step to changing it. The member must also understand the pain the pattern brings so he becomes motivated to change it. The member will then make the desired behavioral changes that will end the pain.

The leader's job is to observe the pattern, and step in to help the member determine the reasons behind it. The leader must continue to observe to see whether the pattern is returning and maintain a policy of zero tolerance if it returns.

13

It Is What It Is

There are many things in the organization that are out of the leader's control. The space is kept safe when the leader knows what her limitations are and can explain this reality to the team. To pretend otherwise is to set up false expectations for success.

Every organization has its political landscape that the leader needs to understand and help members navigate and factor into decision making. Leaders need to openly discuss these issues with teams to help them understand the environment in which they are operating.

As leaders, it can be difficult to admit that we are at times powerless, and that this has nothing to do with our motives or our great ideas. The CEO may have a different agenda that can strip us of the power to get things done or to effect change at an organizational level. Sometimes the CEO wants us to perform only the roles we were hired to do and rejects all ideas outside this scope.

We may not want to admit this lack of power, but it is unwise to pretend we have what we do not. Lack of power isn't permanent; we may get more power by forging alliances with other team leaders or when the organization shifts focus. The leader's job is to keep her finger on the political pulse of the organization to know when there's a political shift that may send more power her way. I accept when I have no power and make my plans anyway, so that when the winds shift I am in position to proceed and act. I stay prepared for any opportunities that present themselves.

The project was agreed upon at the strategic planning session and I was the project sponsor. But the business unit leader who was to benefit from the project rejected it. As a result, the project stalled. Team members wanted to know why I didn't fight for the project to proceed since it had been sanctioned as part of the strategic plan. However, I do not fight to work. When I fight, I lose sight of the purpose of the project and the focus becomes getting the project started, which places the business unit leader in the counterattacking position of getting the project stopped. I cannot win under these conditions, and the options before me were just as unpalatable. I could go to the CEO and have him mandate the business unit (BU) head undertake the project, further offending her and making her even more determined to undermine the success of the project. I could also negotiate with the BU leader, giving her something in exchange for allowing me to do the project, but this weakens my political power in the organization and does not serve me in the long run.

I accepted that I had no control over the situation; I accepted the leader's rejection of the project and worked with another business unit leader who accepted the project.

We have been taught to always win and to get what we want done at all costs. As a result, leaders connive and fight to enact projects that other leaders don't want and they struggle to get the promised success. Leaders with different agendas get involved in the game of "spy vs. spy," developing strategies to get what they want, leaving behind a trail of blood, bitterness, and rancor. The loser is left licking wounds and prepping for the next battle with the victor. Leaders accumulate power by invading the territories of other leaders, sometimes usurping the CEO's power to do so.

I have a lot of power in my sphere and I don't need to invade another leader's territory, nor make someone look bad so that I look good. I look good by the things I do and the wins I get. The wins of other leaders don't bother me; I'm not in competition with them. Instead I focus on the wins of my team; the more they win, the more I win.

Anna wanted to purchase a piece of software and went to the information technology manager to request the purchase without getting her leader's approval. Anna didn't understand the approval for software expenditure was at that time a touchy subject since the annual budget was being greatly reduced. While her leader praised Anna's initiative to move along the idea, he walked her through the intricacies of the situation. While Anna focused on getting the job done, she didn't factor in the wider organizational context. Anna's decision couldn't be faulted, but she needed to work with her leader and consider the bigger picture when executing her ideas.

Projects are shut down for various reasons such as cost, time, methodology, and other reasons that may be known only by the leader. Members need to check in with the leader to ensure the project can leap the organizational hurdles that ordinarily delay execution. I advise my team members that if we're to win, we need to be able to control the project or influence the decision makers, and the project outcome must make an impact and be important. These criteria are used to rank projects and determine which will be pushed to execution.

CONTROL

Michelle developed a training program to help staff manage both personal and work projects. There was a high level of interest from teams across the organization. Yet when she sent out the sign-up sheets, no one committed to attend the sessions. Other team leaders refused to give members time off to attend the training since the team leaders didn't think the program was relevant.

Michelle had total control over designing the program, but the execution—which was measured by attendance—was beyond her sphere of control. Therefore she couldn't win. Eventually, Michelle ran the program during the lunch hour so the leaders' approval wouldn't be needed for execution. When leaders heard about the benefits of the program, they requested the training and Michelle got the win. Michelle should have approached the leaders and sold the benefits of the training program before moving to execution. This would have gotten her to win much quicker.

When leaders identify projects for execution, the first check is to determine if we have the control to execute. If project execution requires resources that the leader cannot acquire, then the leader is not in control of the project. The leaders who have control of the resources are the ones in control of the project since they can jeopardize execution.

The control does not have to be a showstopper; it may mean that we have to find an alternate way of execution, get someone else to champion the idea, or sell the idea to the decision makers. If these alternatives don't work, then we need to walk away from the project regardless of its brilliance.

When I don't have control, I depersonalize the issue and focus on the work. I approach each engagement within the organization as if I were an external consultant working for a client. I work on the premise that the client may or may not accept the project. I do not fight or argue for a project; but I use the numbers, facts, benefits, and research to sell the point. When the project is accepted, I clearly outline the scope of my control and that of the other leaders involved.

If the project is turned down, I assume the arguments presented weren't compelling enough to sell why the work should be done, or I haven't done adequate research, or the client doesn't think the project is worthwhile. I am not annoyed; instead, I start looking for the next opportunity.

INFLUENCE

When we have no direct control, we need to influence the decision makers to get them to approve the project. We have to sell the project's positive impact and added value to the teams that we want to influence. The project must be perceived as beneficial, and able to solve a problem, negate an effect, or improve the way team members work.

When leaders heard attendees praising the training program, they became convinced of the benefits and gave members the time away from their desks to attend the training. The work of the influencer is significant; he may need to change the message for each person and sell what appeals to his particular situation. This is not to be confused with negotiating; I am not exchanging anything to get the leader to change his mind.

IMPORTANCE

Leaders need to ensure that the projects are important to the team, to another team, or to the larger organization. If a project is not important, there is no value in wasting time on it. Winning is not just about completing projects; it's about making a difference to the way we think, the things we do, or how we benefit the organization, the employees, or the clients. There is little point in expending energies just to do something. The result should be something that the team is proud of and can be perceived as important throughout the company.

Michelle's training program could change the way projects are managed across the organization, resulting in higher implementation rates. This was a big win, for her and for me.

SWEATING STUFF

I use these three criteria—control, influence, and importance— to sweat an issue. The levels of control and influence that I will have on a project, and its overall importance, will determine how much energy I'm willing to expend to get the project sanctioned and executed. These criteria also help me determine the priority level of the project.

Projects that I have full control of and are important are the ones that rank highest for execution. The ones that are important and the leader can be easily influenced are second in priority. Any project where influencing is a difficult job is parked for when conditions change, and any project that is of low importance will be done when the team has down time.

I will not fight for a project if I am unsure about its ultimate success. I will not get the CEO to usurp leaders' authority and mandate them to engage the project because then I would have to deal with other leaders' resentment. I will keep talking, persuading, and working with the leaders to help them understand. I will pilot the project in a small group, run tests, and distribute the results so the leaders can see the impact the project can make. I don't sweat when I cannot influence or control; instead, I concentrate on the things I can control and spend my energies there.

I have limited time and limited resources, so I focus on areas that will result in a win. I'm not putting energy into areas where the chances of winning are slim.

CONCLUSION

The work doesn't belong to us. A project isn't supposed to be a source of contention, especially when we accept that there may be other ways of achieving the desired outcome. There is enough work to do in our own teams, yet we fight other leaders to influence what they are doing and go beyond the sphere of our control. When the team leader pretends she has power she doesn't have, she is setting up the team for failure. When the team leader can say, "This is not my area of expertise," the team members are freed up to find additional assistance and do things differently.

When members understand we aren't meant to fight to work, the team grows stronger. The space is violated when leaders give false optimism about situations they can't influence, control, or impact.

Check In Regularly

Keeping the space safe is an ongoing responsibility for the leader. Just as we check the weather report to prepare ourselves for the day ahead, the leader should review the conditions of the safe space before engaging with the team. The safe space is a tool; therefore it must be kept well oiled and maintained on a regular basis to ensure it's effective at helping the team complete projects.

Each member needs to understand what the space is about, why it was created, how to use it, and the rules that govern it. The leader needs to constantly communicate the rationale for the space to reinforce the concept. I check with the team members on an ongoing basis to remind them that the space is there, and although personal issues may come up, the space is foremost about work. The leader needs to regularly evaluate the area to ensure that the message is received and understood.

The first level of evaluation is through observation. What is happening in the space? Are members lingering after a meeting or are they tripping over each other to get out? Who comes to you in the space to explore an idea or a concern, personal or otherwise? What are the body language and atmosphere when the team has meetings?

If team meetings seem tense, members are fidgety and dart out of the room as soon as meetings are over, members can't look at you (unless for cultural reasons), or only some members speak to you privately, then the space is not safe for all members.

After checking my calendar, I noticed that Simon had not scheduled any personal time in the space. This was the first indication that something about the safe space didn't fit well with him. He sat in a position that didn't allow for direct eye contact with me or other team members. I needed to check in with Simon to see what was wrong, understand why, and work to make the space safe for him.

The second level of evaluation is done by listening. What topics are being discussed in the space? Who speaks in the space? What voices are not heard? At meetings, Simon was reserved and quiet. He didn't share other than to report on his work, and he contributed little to group discussions. Other team members hinted that Simon was not comfortable in the space.

The third check is on the content of what is said in the room. What kinds of topics are being discussed there? What challenges are members bringing to the table? Is the team discussing organizational issues that are real and relevant? Are members questioning the status quo? Simon was not participating in any discussions and when asked a direct question, he shrugged.

Chances are if members aren't asking difficult questions or discussing subjects that are taboo in the company, then they probably don't feel safe in the space. When the leader's evaluation indicates that nothing is amiss in the room, the leader regularly reminds the team about the purpose of the space. When the evaluation shows otherwise, the leader works with the members and the team to rectify the situation.

INDIVIDUAL

Humans can be mercurial, which is why the leader needs to communicate regularly with each member of the team. The leader doesn't have to understand the individual triggers and responses, but through observation and listening she can be aware when these are activated so she can limit their effect on other team members and the use of the space.

Each team member is invited to a thirty-minute one-on-one session. These sessions are voluntary and are scheduled by the team member on a bimonthly basis. The member is in charge of the topics and leads the discussion, while the leader holds the space and acts as a coach. The safe space rules apply to these sessions. Ideally, the session is broken down into three ten-minute sections. The first ten minutes are for the member to discuss any work or personal issue of his choice. For the next ten minutes the leader coaches the member on the issues raised, and the last ten minutes are for a summation of the conversation along with the next steps identified by the team member.

While no topic is off limits, the team member needs to appreciate that the session is only about him. This means that members cannot seek information about another member. They can talk about their relationship with another member as long as they take personal responsibility for their roles in the interactions. This is not a question and answer session where members question leaders about the organization or decisions. The leader notes these questions for future discussion with the entire team, so that information is shared with all team members at the same time. If the organizational issue has a personal impact on one member, then it's relevant to the discussion. It often takes several one-on-one sessions for members to understand that the session is only about them. Members who are unaccustomed to receiving this level of attention will try to deflect attention onto other people or issues in the organization. Members who are not accustomed to having direct access to the leader will seek answers to all the burning questions they have.

Leaders need to gently guide members back to the purpose of the session. It is about the member. It is about the person in the room, not anything else.

These meetings offer great insight into the team members and help the leader understand how to motivate and work with them. They allow the leader to check in with team members about how they feel in the space and how the space can be made safe for them.

Members who feel safe regularly come for one-on-one meetings. This is part of their success tool kit that they use to get rid of distractions, plan projects, and take risks.

I invite members who do not volunteer for one-on-one

sessions to meet with me. Simon reluctantly accepted a meeting request and dragged himself into the safe space. I explained
that my motive for meeting with him was to check on whether
he felt safe in the space. He responded that he felt safe but he
wasn't ready for the one-on-one session since in earlier sessions
he had been very emotional. When I asked what was behind the
emotional responses, he replied, "It's something I need to deal
with." I reminded Simon that even though other topics may cross
over, the space was about work and that he could use the space
to improve his work. I also said that the one-on-one slots were
nice to have but certainly not mandatory, so he didn't have to use
the space for that purpose. After our chat, Simon was more participatory in team meetings. Many months later, he scheduled a
one-on-one appointment, saying he felt he was ready to have the
session, since he was more in control of his emotions.

Focused attention and open-ended questions force members
to think and deal with the issues they're grappling with. Powerful,
probing questions help the member to confront hidden issues and
have "aha" moments that wouldn't occur outside the safe space.
By summarizing what a member has said, the leader is essentially
holding up a mirror for the member to see the issue differently.
The space allows members to step away from the minutiae of
the day to day and adopt another vantage point to unearth new
issues or connect the dots of certain situations. Most of us don't
have the luxury of stopping and thinking with undivided, non-
judgmental attention. In fact, this attention can be overwhelming
and that's what causes the emotional reaction of members. Some
of them find it fascinating while others are scared.

There will be times when members don't use the space, and

leaders shouldn't coerce them into using it. Members will return to the space, though not always for a structured one-on-one session. They'll pop in for fifteen minutes to discuss a problem they're having, to vent about personal or other issues, to bounce an idea off the leader, to get help solving a problem, or to share a success. The one-on-one meetings set the tone for these interactions, since the format and the safety are identical.

TEAM

I meet with my team each Monday morning to set goals, check in on work, answer any questions that are pertinent to the team, and to divulge information about the organization. These meetings are also governed by the set team rules. Each team member reports on the progress of the projects, describes where he or she needs help, and sets milestones for completion. The meeting morphs into a general discussion about whatever the team wants to speak about. Sometimes the members want to share good news, learn a technique, discuss what's happening in the organization; and other times the members just want to return to their desks. These meetings can last from thirty minutes to two hours according to the team's needs.

These meetings aren't always comfortable since I ask about the reasons behind decisions made and challenge members to take responsibility, tackle bigger challenges, and think outside the box. I ask open-ended questions that initially made members squirm. Some team members disagreed with my approach since they thought that questioning should be done privately. I explain that I ask the questions so I won't make assumptions about the reasons certain decisions have been made. I ask questions without the intention of blaming and for clarity. The team can learn from each other's mistakes and successes while observing the types of questions they can use to assist each other in decision making beyond the room. My intention is never to denigrate members, and they are invited to give me feedback if they suspect I am mistreating a member. Some members still don't agree with this approach and act as a barometer for my behavior.

Whenever a member gets defensive or begins to take the questioning personally, I remind members that my motive is for them to think and solve problems on their own. This statement relieves the tension immensely. Team members may be offended when they are the ones in the spotlight, but when it's someone else's turn, they realize that my questioning isn't personal. It focuses on the work, the decisions, the lessons learned, and the next steps.

At team meetings, I check in with the team as a group on how the space has worked for them and what is needed to keep it safe. Occasionally we review the rules and the purpose of the space so that we are always focused on the reason for the session.

CONCLUSION

The safe space may bring a level of discomfort to the team members who are being held personally accountable for what they do and say. Most people want someone else to answer a question or tell them what to do, whereas this style calls upon the member to provide his own answer. When a member says to me, "What should I do?" I repeat the question back to him, "What should you do?" Team members have confessed they find this type of questioning to be annoying, as it forces them to think when they really just wanted an answer; but now they agree the technique has helped them become better decision makers and empowered them to make effective decisions every day.

Initially, I had to be patient and refrain from giving answers; I learned to maintain the discipline of leading team members to their own discovery. I had to be deliberate in my openness and trustworthiness and consistent in my behavior to ensure I always asked questions and pushed the team to learn. I had to constantly communicate my motive, listen, observe, and have difficult conversations with team members. These are not the fun parts of the job, but they are critical for the success of the team and by extension my success. As a leader, I need to know what's going on so I can help the members win; therefore I need to understand their fears and help them remove obstacles that keep them from succeeding. It's not easy for members or for leaders, but it's well worth the continued effort.

The Safe Space Can Backfire

The safe space is an environment for taking risks that could lead to big wins. It recognizes that members have personal lives that at times may encroach on their professional lives. It provides a room for members to park personal issues so they can focus on their work projects.

In the safe space, Celia opened up about the difficult relationship she had with her teenage son and the concerns that kept her up at night. In the space, she determined some action steps she could take to minimize her stress and determine the boundaries that she would set for her son. When Celia continued to deliver poor quality work, I had a chat with her. She was annoyed and told me that she had been "vulnerable" in the room as she shared deeply about the things that mattered to her and yet I couldn't give her a break. I explained to Celia that the safe space was about clearing a space for her to work but it wasn't about giving excuses for the poor quality of her work.

The confidentiality rule says that information shared in the room stays in the room and won't be used to judge Celia or her work. Celia remained baffled for months. While she attended team meetings and respected the rules, she no longer had one-on-one sessions with me. In a feedback session, she said that she found me cold and aloof and that she didn't understand how, after she had shared her personal story, I could just focus on the work and not cut her some slack.

I hadn't anticipated this type of reaction since team members more or less accepted that sharing personal information was a way of clearing space for work. Celia assumed that because she had shared her deeply personal story, I would then be more forgiving when she produced poor quality work. She wanted high levels of sympathy and was dissatisfied with empathy. She wanted me to throw her a pity party with work as the confetti. She didn't accept that the safe space was primarily about work.

Sharing something personal is taking a big risk. I respect the conversations that members share, and I hold them in deepest confidence and congratulate the member's bravery and move on. Members open up to me and I hold the space for them to explore the situation, ask them questions that will help them get to the other side of the issue, and move on.

When Celia shared, we made decisions about her workload and the type of tasks on which she could focus. The sharing helped me understand her struggle; yet while I may be empathetic, it doesn't mean that I will cut her any slack.

Each team member has personal burdens to carry, and he or

she shares them to varying degrees. Members know I am available to listen, won't judge them, and that they're free to unburden so they can work. The space is not a place to give excuses for poor work performance.

SPACE VIOLATION

The space is violated when members, the team as a collective, or the leader shirks responsibility for keeping the space safe.

Members

Team members are the holders of the space. It was created for their use and is a tool to help them achieve their objectives. It can backfire in different ways:

- Breaking the agreed-upon rules. For me, one of the most serious breaches of the space is when team members break the confidentiality they hold for each other. This removes their ability to trust the space, and it can take the team a long time to recover from broken trust. The team needs to be involved in sanctioning the guilty member(s), since the team set up the rules. The team determines whether it feels safe with the offending member present, and the team decides if it wants to exclude the member from private discussions. I abide by its decisions.

- Misunderstanding the purpose of discussions. Some members remain fixated on the discussions held in the space and forget the motive of the space is to help the team win. These members may expect the leader to cut them slack because of what's said in the space. Instead, each member needs to revisit the motive for telling his story. Is it to clear up a space so work can happen? Is it to unburden himself to create room for work to happen? Is he inviting the team leader to a pity party? Is he creating excuses for non-performance?

- Creating lowered expectations. A member may anticipate that lower quality work will be excused because of what she shares in the safe space. However, in the safe space life is viewed as a continuum with no real separation between personal and work lives. The space therefore helps members maintain balance between the two and ensures that best efforts continue, despite what may be happening in their personal lives.

- Avoiding personal responsibility. It can be tempting to shun ownership of one's role in negative situations, and view these as someone else's problem. Enforcing use of "I" statements should help all members take responsibility for their roles.

- Fearing failure. These members need to change the way they view situations before they can embrace the idea of failing. When Susan, a self-described perfectionist, embraced failure as a learning mechanism, she had less anxiety about its occurrence.

- Clinging to the need to be right. These people will

go to great lengths to stray from the truth and force untrue results to make themselves right. This is a difficult habit to break since it's often a personal safety mechanism.

- Failing to apologize or make amends. These members don't understand the impact of their actions as they often cannot grasp that they've offended others. When this occurs, the issue is discussed at team meetings. If the member still fails to recognize the problem, the discussion ends. Team members usually realize their wrongdoing after the meeting and make amends as team members continue the conversation and sanction the member.

- Misinterpreting comments by making them personal. People can be petty and super sensitive, and make every situation about themselves. They don't want to hear the truth, and they'll deflect things pertaining to them onto someone else. They make it uncomfortable for other team members to speak the truth by twisting their statements into personal insults. Other team members walk on eggshells around these super-sensitive team members, and often end up limiting or even curtailing their conversations with them. As a result, these types never get much-needed feedback and stay in a bubble, missing out on critical reality checks regarding their behavior or work. Other team members need to be encouraged to continue being open and honest with these members, even if it feels unrewarding.

- Complaining about work. Some members complain about everything and everyone, thus creating a stressful and burdensome environment and making it difficult for the team to work.

- Gossiping and destroying trust. If one person gossips and others join in, this erodes trust and makes it even harder to gain it back. Confidentiality is critical to the safe space, and all members need to understand and respect this.

- Disrupting the stability of the space with major personal issues. The space is compromised when a member's personal problems are bigger than the work and he becomes unable to concentrate on the tasks at hand. This member's instability can disrupt the stability of the space and make it unpredictable. I recommend that these people take time off or be given some lighter duties until their personal situation clears up.

Some team members link the sharing of personal tales to friendship and expect the leaders to take a personal interest in them based on what they've shared in the space. Franca was annoyed. She told me that the relationship I shared with Sandra, another team member, was a close and personal one and she didn't understand why we didn't have the same relationship, especially after she'd shared personal information with me in the safe space. I asked her to think about topics I discussed with Sandra. But Franca had no answer.

"Do I speak about her husband?" I asked.

"No," Franca said.

"Do I speak about her in-laws?"

"No," she said.

"Do I speak about her kids?"

"No."

"What do I speak about?" I asked.

"Work," she replied sheepishly.

I asked, "What makes you think we're friends?"

Franca paused, and said, "Well, you talk and laugh with her."

"Yes," I said, "Sandra's personality makes it easy for me to have a rapport with her; it is what it is. We are not friends. We only have work in common."

I make a point of speaking to team members only about work. I never ask about their personal life outside of the safe space unless they have shared with everyone about a specific personal event such as a wedding, vacation, or illness. Friendship is organic and can't be forced; it's not a leadership trait.

Members who confuse being friendly with friendship will compare the rapport levels between the leader and team members. When they demand that the relationships be replicated with them, they are violating the space, since they are subtly charging the leader with favoritism.

Members who want and do not get personal attention from the leaders may feel betrayed and lose interest in the space. I would invite these members to meet me for a one-on-one meeting. This becomes a balancing act for me. While I refuse to indulge members who appear needy, I am aware that team members have unique personalities and need to be treated differently. When I realized how important it was for some members to show me pictures from personal celebrations, I acquiesced. It was a small compromise to make for the members to continue to feel safe.

A member will display any or all of these behaviors from time to time and will then need a nudge to realize that he is making the space unsafe. These occasions are usually short-lived, and the problem is usually solved when the behavior is mirrored to the member. Any member who constantly displays the above-mentioned behaviors might have chronic patterns that reside beyond the leader's ability to manage. If these behaviors continue, both the leader and the team need to determine if the space can ever be safe with these members, and should decide how to protect the space from the member. Remedies may include counseling, coaching, exclusion from discussions, or sanctions, and at the extreme, transfer out of the team.

I accept that the space will at times feel unsafe for team members. Any person who cannot receive feedback, who views the world through a defensive lens, who needs to be told things in a sensitive manner, who doesn't want to hear anything negative, who's not open to criticism, and who needs to be right will not find the space safe. I can live with this situation. I will continue to hold out an invitation for these members to use the space if or when they want to.

Leaders

Leaders are the gatekeepers of the space, and as such have the primary responsibility for keeping it safe. Leaders make the space unsafe when they:

- Make assumptions based on what members share in the space, thus violating the confidentiality rules.

- Give personal advice to members and get personally involved in members' lives. The premise on which the space was created—that adults know how to and can solve problems—is violated.

- Exert their egos, and tell members how to behave.

- Gossip about team members and share confidential information.

- Do not give honest feedback to members.

- Do not use tact when giving brutally honest feedback.

- Use euphemisms since, as with all lies, these undermine trust and are difficult to recover from.

- Have favorites and treat members differently.

- Display inconsistent behavior, which makes the space unpredictable.

- Do not want to be challenged by members.

- Want members to do as they say without question. (Only when members can question and challenge will the space be truly safe.)

- Coerce or bribe members to take action. I do not subscribe to the idea of applying pressure or force to help teams achieve their best. Members will achieve what they believe is possible and what rewards them.

- Pit members against each other.

- Use annual bonuses as a whipping tool.

- Stop thinking about the team and think only of themselves.

- Make decisions so that they (leaders) will look good or save face.

- Stop listening.

- Blame members for mistakes, which will prevent others from taking risks.

- Avoid assuming leadership of the team. While members can be involved in decision making and the leader should consider their opinions, the buck stops with the leader.

- Do not make decisions.

- Do not intervene and halt inappropriate behavior.

- Shy away from difficult situations.

- Do not step in to settle problems or team issues.

Team members expressed their exasperation with Andrew. He was unable to accept any feedback about his behavior and how it affected the members. He thought they were jealous or didn't like him. From my observations at team meetings and the snippets of conversations I overheard, I knew I had to get involved. I was brutally honest with Andrew and mirrored his behavior and the impact it had on the team. He didn't take kindly to my comments, but there was no other way to deal with him than being very direct. This created an opening for other team members to share the truth with Andrew and to bring some sort of level-headedness to the playing field. When Andrew continued his behavior, I referred him to the internal coaching program for assistance.

Leaders can be self-delusional because we all believe we're doing a great job. A 180-degree evaluation conducted by the human resources department or an outside consultant can provide feedback about our leadership abilities. A coach can also help us figure out the issues and handle them when they arise.

Team

Anything that dishonors the creativity and intelligence of the team and prevents it from improving its status quo is an act that contradicts the purpose of the safe space.

Team violations occur when the team:

- Consciously or unconsciously collaborates to violate the rules of the space. Each team member had a complaint about Andrew; yet when members evaluated his behavior they gave him high scores. When confronted with the results, they admitted that independently each person decided it wasn't worth the effort to rate Andrew since he couldn't value the feedback and would have a negative reaction to the ratings. When the team actively colludes to or is complicit in perpetuating an untruth about a situation (as with Andrew's feedback), the space becomes unsafe because the team is operating on a false premise. When the team pretends that everything is fine and that all team members get along when they don't, the space has been violated.

- Ignores each member's right to confidentiality. When I informed Jo of her much anticipated promotion, I didn't inform the other team members. It was not their business. If their reaction was to demand that Jo or I tell them about the promotion or felt we were keeping secrets, the space would have been violated for both Jo and me.

- Tries to resolve issues among the group and doesn't alert the leader about problems. If members had alerted me about the problems they were having with Andrew, I might have been able to intervene earlier. Because the safe space allows members to take initiatives, they may try to assist each other with personal situations even though they don't have a complete picture of the situation.

- Expects each member to conform to a norm that has nothing to do with the team rules. We feel more comfortable when we belong to a group that thinks and acts the same, but this is not the purpose of the space.

We celebrate the individuality of the members. All we ask is that they follow the rules they co-created.

- Coerces members to behave, dress, or speak in a certain way. This crushes personal creativity, and strips the member of the freedom to be himself. The member will feel discriminated against.

- Forces members to follow the rules. This dishonors the member's intelligence. Each member has to make a personal choice to follow the rules; most members will willingly accept and adhere to the rules since they created them, and will also accept sanctions when they break the rules.

- Allows conflict to get out of hand. Conflict encourages members to exchange and discuss opposing views. Discussions help members recognize that the resolution doesn't have to be "my way" or "your way." It is not a win-win; it's not a win-lose. New meaning can be created if we think my way *and* your way, meaning that we consider all ideas and examine the good in each suggestion. When we don't fight to be right, we gain an opportunity to let different ideas breed different thinking, thus creating a magical solution that didn't exist before.

- Refuses to get to the source of irritation. When members avoid digging deep to find the inciting incident, conflict remains unresolved. Cindy confided her problems with me to Christian and Petra. Christian acted as a dam, storing all of Cindy's feelings to provide her with temporary relief that would be lost when she left his presence. Petra listened and relayed Cindy's problems to me. I couldn't act on what I heard since the confidentiality rules didn't allow me to speak or act on what Petra said. Both Petra and Christian needed to direct Cindy to me as the conflict was between us. They were trying to help but in the long run, they made matters worse. Each team member needs to resolve issues directly with the member with whom they have issues.

The leader and members should regularly discuss how the space is working and identify any violations. An external facilitator was invited to host an open and honest feedback forum for the team. This was a revealing and somewhat unpleasant experience for everyone. The session highlighted some of the misconceptions about the space and allowed us to create some new rules. After the session, we reviewed the positive things that came out of the session, recounted what we learned, and summarized what we'd do differently going forward. We then modified the rules to enshrine the new knowledge that will help us avoid past pitfalls.

CONCLUSION

Space violations need to be addressed. They will not go away. While team members assist in noting violations, the onus is on the leader to be vigilant and deal with them when they occur. The leader needs to self-reflect on her actions to ensure she is not a source of violation.

Some members may never view the space as safe. They may see it as a management trick that allows the leader to extract work from the member even when the member is facing personal turmoil or not operating at his best. And they may be right.

Different Strokes

Most mornings when I arrive at work, I fetch my keys and head straight to my office. I purposefully make limited contact with staff until I have settled in my office and recovered from the effort it takes to get dressed, face the morning commute, and make it to the office at a reasonable time. This is the way I prepare myself to get ready for the day ahead.

But Sheila was very offended. She thought I was rude for not saying, "Good morning" as I passed by her desk to get to my office. I was baffled and peeved by her view. I thought I had a right to choose how I started my morning, including whether I extended a greeting. It became a silent battle as I made a point of not saying "Good morning."

Eventually a member confronted me. "Why can't you just say, 'Good morning,' if that's what she needs?" That forced me to think. My ego had gotten involved and created a minefield around a non-issue, and my ability to keep the space safe was being questioned because I was refusing to compromise. I resolved then to greet people when I entered the office. It was such a small thing for me to give so that another member could feel safe.

Each leader needs to figure out what little gesture he could do that would really signal to all the team members that he's committed to making them safe. That was a hard lesson for me. I know now that I can violate the safe space by not respecting what seem to be small needs of each member.

I don't like negotiating or compromising, but at times the space calls for just that. When I weigh the compromise against the long-term efforts, I confess that it doesn't take much from me and the rewards far outweigh the effort.

Performance measurement reviews provide more of these types of challenges for me as the leader. Each year, Sharon received great reviews and bonuses, but she hadn't been promoted and didn't understand why. When she transferred to my team I spoke to her previous team leader, who explained that while Sharon's work was of high quality, she was unable to multitask. He thought she stayed in analysis paralysis mode and couldn't make a decision. I asked him if he'd ever told her this and he said no. I sat with Sharon and told her exactly why she was not promoted and she was reduced to tears. She was angry and hurt since she had often been praised for her work.

Luckily Sharon is a practical woman. When asked if there was any truth in the statement, she admitted there was. She developed a plan, worked hard to change her behavior, and a year later she received the promotion she wanted and deserved.

Not all employees are like Sharon. Her willingness to overcome adversity reflected her desire to be promoted. She understood that the choices before her were either accept the feedback and work to address it, or deny it and remain stuck in the same place at the next performance review.

Like Sharon, Simone was a transfer who had not received a promotion for several years. Her previous team leader outlined that he kept Simone's tasks at a rudimentary level since she did not seem able to handle more than this, and she did not readily accept feedback from her peers. Simone was upset and rejected the negative feedback I gave about her inability to be promoted. She considered it a personal attack since her former team leader gave her only positive feedback. She did not question the negative correlation between good reviews and no promotions. Six months later at the next performance review, the previous comments were still relevant since Simone did not accept any opportunities to get involved in projects that she considered outside of her job specifications; and she was still not a team player. Simone remained hurt by the negative feedback and was stuck in her emotional response; she hadn't moved to accept the facts of the feedback. I had to ask questions such as: "What result do you want from your next performance evaluation?" "How will you benefit from a better evaluation?" "What do you want your peers to think of you?" and "How can I help you?" to help her see the opportunities before her and understand my role was to assist her to achieve a better result. Together, we identified projects that she could get involved in, training she could attend, and negative behaviors she could work on limiting. This was not an easy exercise for either of us. Simone was reluctant to commit to an action plan, unsure about attending workshops, and uncertain that she could change her behavior. I was frustrated that she couldn't readily see the benefits of making what I considered small changes, and that I needed to hold her hand throughout the entire planning process. Over time, as we worked together, she made the desired changes.

Some team members are self-motivated. They want to do their best, and once they understand the obstacles in their path to success they willingly and determinedly work to remove and overcome them. These members view the leader as their support system and, regardless of how they feel about the leader, will progress.

Those in need of external motivation will rely on the leader. Their feelings about the leader and the relationship they share with that leader are important factors to their success.

While I prefer to work with more independent team members, I recognize the needs of the more dependent and temper my impatience to provide them with the motivation they need.

IT'S A MATTER OF TRUST

When I reflect on those two feedback sessions, I know there are other factors that were responsible for the difference in the two responses. Sharon had a greater level of trust in me as the leader. We shared a professional relationship before she joined my team, and I had commended her on her work many times before. She believed my motive was genuine and that I wanted her to succeed and receive a promotion. The hurtful feedback was tempered by the trust she had in me and my motive, and she could take the comments on board.

Simone, however, didn't have the same level of trust in me. She had a high rework factor and at times was exasperated by the demanding standards I had set for the quality of work. She saw the feedback as another source of criticism, as she didn't trust my motive; as a result, she rejected the feedback. But as her levels of trust in me increased, she implemented the recommendations.

IT'S NOT WHAT, BUT HOW

I also had to accept partial responsibility for the fallout from the feedback sessions. Before meeting with either member, I focused on my intention to "give honest feedback," targeted toward completion of the task. I didn't consider what I wanted as the outcome after feedback. If my intention had been set as "after the session each member will take the feedback on board and make the relevant changes," I would have considered the individual differences between the two members (such as level of personal motivation, emotional intelligence, trust in me and my motive), and paid more attention to "how" the feedback was delivered. I would have tailored my words for each person and I would have spoken to each individual in a manner that suited each person's needs.

Now whenever I give negative feedback, I declare aloud to the team member that the motive behind giving feedback is to build a future state where the problem doesn't exist, and I check that the team member agrees this is the focus of the session. While this doesn't absolve me from tailoring the information to suit the personalities involved, it does allow me some wiggle room as I become less central to the equation.

SELF-EVALUATION BY THE LEADER

Before I go into the performance evaluations with my team members, I get myself ready. I focus on being aware of and honest about my feelings and how this may impact the feedback. I make certain that I'm not showing any biases that would prevent me from being fair and honest. If I'm having a bad day or I'm not in a neutral state about the issue of the member, I don't offer feedback.

I ask myself what traits about the person both annoy and please me. For those traits that bother me, I generate a list and then drill down into the details of what needs to change in order for me to change my answer. This makes me aware of whether I'm unfairly ascribing qualities to the member or issue. Sometimes I will call a friend and vent so I can get to a place of clarity before I give feedback.

The leader needs to recognize that although the members are treated the same in the space, each team member is unique and has different needs. I thought that because the playing field was even I could ignore the individuality of the members. I thought that I could ignore those who were hesitant about the space and pay attention only to those who were enthusiastic about the space. I had to remind myself that I was leading each and every member of the team and that the safe space was for all of them. I needed to respect the individuality of each member for the space to be truly safe for all. As such, I could not treat them the same. I had to celebrate their differences even when it went against my grain.

Leaders need to motivate the people with whom they work according to their needs and abilities. Some members may need a private pep talk before they can get started, while others may need a different form of personal attention. If leaders want everyone on board, then sometimes they have to do the outreach. It's not my personal style, but I've seen how not reaching out to reluctant, hesitant, or scared members can impact negatively on the space.

CONCLUSION

The leader's challenge is to remember that although all members are equal in the space, members are individuals with different personalities and different needs. Leaders need to change their tactics when they deal with each of the members.

17

What's in It for Me?

For me, working is one of the ways in which I fulfill my personal vision of daily "enhancing the lives of the people with whom I come into contact." Each year I review the things I've done to determine what else I need to do to achieve this vision. In the working world, this translates to building my personal profile—whether for an online presence, a networking opportunity, or the traditional resume. When I worked on contract jobs that offered no spectacular opportunities, I attended a training program each year and worked in my chosen field outside the organization. My personal vision continues to influence the choices I make and the jobs I accept.

I assume that team members are like me; they want and deserve more, and are working to achieve some self-fulfilling purpose. As a result, I suggest that they aren't just coming to work to do a job, but they're also adding to their life experience and building their personal profiles. Their current roles are stepping-stones to furthering their personal agenda, whether that may be a position they want, or a bigger spot with an impressive salary and benefits to match. Each task can be an accomplishment, or close a skills gap so achievements may be amassed. Team members need to perform with the belief they're readying themselves for the next opportunity—within or external to the company—that will take them one step closer to their dreams.

As a result, the team focuses on achievements and on execution. While all ideas and plans are welcomed, they only add to our personal profiles when completed, evaluated, and considered appropriate. The promise of a personal profile packed with achievements that translate to meeting career or other personal objectives provides the ultimate motivation for the team to buy into the safe space. This is a personal benefit that's created by full participation in the space. The members have the leader's support to take risks, and therefore they have the potential to achieve major accomplishments to move closer to their personal goals in a shorter period of time.

Whenever a team member is promoted, resigns for a better paying job, or develops so he is regarded as an expert, the team has a renewed sense of faith in the safe space. The formula has been proven, and the space has shown that it is a place for excellence and growth for the members. (Even employees who are close to retirement can see the benefit. The higher their monthly salaries, the larger their pension benefit.)

SETTING PERSONAL VISION

Perhaps you're one of the lucky ones. You have a personal vision and have been assiduously working the plan. It is your sense of shrewd planning that has made you a leader. What about the people who work for you? Everyone on your team has the requisite qualities and experiences for the assigned job, but how many members have a plan? Could you share the actions that worked for you with your team members? What if you told them to develop a personal vision to see if their jobs fit with their goals?

Team leaders often pay lip service to team members when they say they want to see the members get promoted. Often these are empty, paternalistic statements. The leader can only want what is best for each member if the leader knows what the member wants. Sadly, members often cannot articulate what they want since they have not considered their future or don't know how to talk about their goals. The leader can make an important impact on the member's career choices by helping him frame his personal vision.

PEOPLE WHO DON'T FIT WILL LEAVE

When Devon developed his personal vision, he admitted that the most important thing in his life at that time was making money; he wanted and needed material things. He was newly married and wanted to provide a home for his family. He quit his job and took a contract offer that provided high rewards for long hours. Stating his personal vision helped him realize that a stable job was not generating the income needed to achieve his personal goals. If he stayed on it would have become impossible to motivate him, since the job was incapable of providing the salary he needed. We parted on amicable terms, and he continues to keep me updated on his progress.

I think the best gift a leader can give himself and, by extension, the team is to help each member set a personal vision. This makes it easy for both member and leader to get a clear idea of what the member wants to achieve in terms of work or non-work goals and to make adjustments on the job that will help her achieve these goals. A job then has purpose and it is seen as a stepping-stone or for learning new skills to achieve her vision.

Leaders have a unique perspective on the members. When we understand their vision, we need to admit they may be better off somewhere else, on another team, or at another company. It's our duty to release them. We won't suffer. Other talented members will have a personal vision that aligns with the team's goals and will stay on to contribute. The synergy created when personal visions are aligned with the team's goals generates an amazing energy that propels the team forward toward outstanding performance.

If you get a kick out of helping people, you should help your team members clarify their personal vision and even help them leave if that's necessary for them to reach their goals. They will sing your praises as the leader who was big enough to lead them to success by letting them go.

PEOPLE WHO ARE JUST GETTING BY CAN BE CHALLENGED

Setting the personal visions can be a terrible exercise for people who have never thought about goals, have given up on their dreams, or seem to want nothing from life.

Chris was a dependable person who never complained and followed instructions well. No task was too demeaning; no job too small as long as he received detailed instructions and the task took place within the prescribed hours of work so he could leave the office on time. I could not foresee a role for him on the team. He had no qualifications and displayed no interest in learning a particular skill.

When Chris set his vision, he revealed that he wanted to be a teacher but gave up that dream when his mom got ill. I was relieved. We could now develop a role, assign tasks, and provide training that matched his interests and talents. Chris now conducts training and manages meetings throughout the organization.

The leader may need to find other ways to prompt a response since not all members can express what they want. Anna was highly creative, semi-skilled young woman who willingly did as told. If you needed a poster made, an event planned, or some groceries purchased, she did the job. She often commented that her personal life offered more than her professional life and she was willing to suffer through the working hours to return to her family at the end of the day. Anna's vision was to be a good wife and mother.

Instead of talking vision, I asked, "How do you feel about

your job?" Anna got very quiet and revealed that she had no feel-ings about her job.

I then asked, "Are you proud of the work that you do?"

"No," she said.

I continued, "How do you want your kids to feel about the work that you do?" No response.

"When they ask you about your job, what will you say?" I asked. Again, she didn't respond.

"What needs to change for you to be proud of your job? What would it be like if you could bring your kids to the office and say this is what Mommy does?"

The image of her children not being proud of what she did struck a chord for Anna. A few months after that conversation, she said that she wanted to do more on the job and worked to become the company's expert at Customer Service, which was a strategic differentiator for that company.

Leaders may find the catalyst to spring people into wanting more from their position from the information gleaned during the personal one-on-one sessions. This material has to be tact-fully used since confidentiality means the leader cannot directly bring up the member's issues. Leaders can change the way mem-bers view their jobs when they provide the right motivators.

Leaders need to help team members achieve their vision, even when they're misaligned with the team's work. People remember those who help them achieve their goals and you never know who will help you in the future.

PEOPLE MAY WANT YOUR JOB

Be prepared for the member whose personal vision is to have your job. Do not be shocked by this response; it is not necessarily a bad thing. There is a story about a police sergeant who wanted a promotion but every year he was denied. After the fifth year, he asked why he was denied the promotion. After all, he had done all the right things and his evaluations were great. He was then told there was no one to replace him.

Leaders who want to lead a team to infinity need to check what they are holding on to and why. They may have to revisit their personal visions. If you don't have a successor, then you have nowhere to go. I see leaders walking around the office thinking they're indispensable and no one could do their job, feeling good because they have effectively negated the competition by denying members' opportunities and training. Every time the leader undermines team members, saying they have no new ideas or aren't ready for a promotion, she's really saying she's going to lead this team forever.

This leader is myopic. Her fixation on the status quo means she isn't scanning for opportunities, and if one were to present itself, she wouldn't be in a position to embrace it because she's too busy holding on to what she currently has.

If a team member wants my job, then it's time to assess her readiness and provide training to close any skill gaps. While the organization doesn't need two of us, it may need someone whose skills are complementary for another position, or she may consider moving on to a similar position elsewhere. Working with the member prevents me from being stabbed in the back or having my authority undermined. The team member who wants my job signals that I need to do an honest self-assessment. If I were to apply for my job now, would I be qualified for it?

When someone on my team is a serious contender for my job, then it may be time for me to raise my game by going beyond my regular responsibilities and seeking ways to add unique value to the organization. According to the political landscape and the rumblings of my peers, the member's statement about wanting my job may signal that it's time for me to move on from the company or job. It may also indicate that I need to set my sights higher.

If the leader is at the top of her game, no one else can do her job. My team members have MBAs and I don't; yet I'm not threatened by their qualifications. I generously share with them while always improving my own skills.

ROLE DEVELOPMENT

When members develop and share their vision, a foundation for role development is established. The roles can be aligned to personal vision or be a stretch goal for the member who adds real value to the team and by extension to the company.

I don't want job descriptions for my team members. I want roles, meaty roles that will make team members excited at the prospect of achieving the description of such a lofty job. They should be thrilled as they realize just how big their tiny little job could be. The role holds out the possible achievements for personal profile building and allows them to work creatively and intelligently.

I don't want to think about what needs to be done and give detailed instructions. I don't want to pull my weight and someone else's. I want every member of my team to be equal, with responsibilities matched to his competence, and my expectation is that each person makes the same effort according to his abilities.

Leaders need to develop the members' roles. This cannot be left to the HR department because it doesn't have the vision you have for your team. While HR can frame the roles within the organizational context, the leader is solely responsible for how the available resources are used.

Roles also offer a path for promotions and annual salary increases. When the leader hasn't thought about the member's role beyond the current function, there is no reason to promote her. There's no position into which she could be promoted, since the emphasis has only been placed on her current job. The employee needs to be seen as performing a role that emphasizes the mastery of activities and tasks. Even roles at the lowest rung of the organizational structure can have levels of competency built into them so that when they're mastered, the member can be promoted out of that role and into a position leading to a career path. If the leader hasn't thought beyond the job or looked at the development of the role and the extension of that role in three to five years (according to the complexity), then the member will never be promoted and could remain in the same job forever.

In thinking about the team's vision, I answer these questions:

What do I want to achieve with my team?

What are some of the roles necessary to achieve this?

What do I want to be remembered for in the organization?

How can I organize the work so that people in the department have things to do and can add real meaning to the team?

What will make a difference?

Can the jobs be combined or should they remain separate?

I then meet with members to align personal vision to the team vision and to develop the roles. Roles are set so that members, with training and skill development, can grow into the new roles; they now have a clear goal to strive to reach. The roles clearly identify what types of achievements are expected.

My team is composed of a group of people who have various levels of skills and abilities. I clearly distinguish the doing roles (those which keep the operations going) from the thinking roles (those which have more strategic intent) and ensure that each member is challenged to the best of his abilities.

As members develop and the organization changes, the leader needs to review, extend, or retire roles as necessary. It's not an easy job; it requires a lot of thought as the leader fits the roles together to ensure the team's vision is achieved.

When I joined the company as a strategic planner, we set up the roles to achieve the set vision. After one year, I realized there were huge opportunities to raise the profile of my role and that of the team. As a result, the process improvement role morphed into a process auditor's role with responsibility for documentation. Two new roles were added, and when the incumbent project manager was promoted, her role was eliminated.

Team members no longer see their jobs in a vacuum; the role is in direct relation to their personal vision and what they want. Excellence at their roles will lead to an enhanced personal profile as an inroad to the next big job or big opportunity, within or outside the company.

I tell the team that I expect to work with them in their current roles for no more than three years. My expectation is they will develop completely new roles, and then move out of the team or out of the organization. Just as I'm looking for my next break within or outside of the company, I assume the same is true for the team members.

The team may stumble as new members fill vacated roles, but I can choose from the cream of the crop to replace the departed team members. After all, who doesn't want to work with a leader whose team members all have great track records?

CONCLUSION

All of us directly or indirectly received assistance along the way from people who inspired us, gave us advice, or actually helped us. Whatever breaks you received in your career, you should gladly pass them on. You may be the only one who holds out the possibility that the member is worth something or is doing something worthwhile. The leader needs to show the member that he can excel at his job and move on to even bigger roles within or outside your company.

Leader's Rights and Expectations

The assumption that we all have equal rights in the safe space doesn't always hold true. As the holder of the space, the leader needs to refrain from inappropriate behavior so that the space remains safe. Situations sometimes get the better of me and I don't always want to act like an adult. On occasion, I want to scream at a member or make sarcastic remarks, but I refrain from doing so by remembering how much work it would be to make amends, and how hard it would be to rectify the violations of the space.

We leaders have a right to our emotions and we need to deal with our fears about the risks we take to win. We have real concerns, both personal and professional, that can prevent us from doing our best. However, the safe space may not be the right place for us to deal with our issues.

Ideally, the space is a two-way street with the exchange happening for both the team leader and the members. In reality, this doesn't happen because the team looks up to the leader and not every member is equipped to deal with the leader's frailties. I carefully select the issues I bring to the space so I can mirror the use of the space to the team members. This allows me to show my humanity and builds the level of trust in the space. I think it's dangerous for leaders to bring highly sensitive issues to the space (personal or professional). While every leader will have to make a determination about what can be discussed in general, leaders will need to reflect on the strength of the relationship with the team members and the maturity of the members to determine what issues can be shared. The leader should also consider whether he would be able to look directly at team members after sharing a particular story or whether he is comfortable with team members sharing his story among themselves. The playing field is uneven, and while members are free to use the space however they want, the leader needs to balance what is shared in the room with the silent expectations the team and the organization have for leaders. It helps for leaders to remind themselves of the purpose of the safe space: it was created by the team for members' use, not primarily for the leader's use.

DRAWING THE LINES

Leaders need to set boundaries for team members. My office is the safe space, and it's also where I work. To protect my time, I ask members to set appointments to speak to me. If they don't schedule time, they can drop in any time for fifteen minutes. But when those fifteen minutes are over, I boot them out of my office without apology.

I close my office door to signal that I've blocked off time to complete assignments, follow up on calls, or have some alone time; coworkers understand I am not to be interrupted unless it's urgent—which means it's a matter of life or death or the company is about to lose millions.

Initially, members knocked until I explained that when my door is shut I won't welcome any interruptions; they can send me an email or wait until I have an opening. Members have learned to appreciate that I need time alone, and now they, too, carve out time for themselves to work uninterrupted.

I set boundaries for my office to maintain the integrity of the space and to ensure that I can fully support team members when they need to use the space. Boundaries tell others when and how to respect my time and that of others who may need to use the space.

My unavailability has led members to solve problems with their peers, and I have become a port of last resort when a problem arises.

As a leader, I set the tone for the team's relationship when I set personal boundaries. Team members can't comment on my physical appearance unless it's to provide a compliment, and I do the same with them. I believe people have a right to their personal style, and as long as it's deemed by the organization as office appropriate, members are free to carry themselves as they wish.

Boundaries set the scope of the safe space. Leaders should set the boundaries that tell members how and when to use the space.

LEADER'S RIGHTS

As a leader, I have the right to be seen and heard. I will state my opinion in all discussions, ask questions for clarity, and ask for help when needed. I expect that team members will actively listen to me as I do to them.

I have the right to discretion. I can give concessions to staff without setting precedents or being accused of displaying favoritism. When a member is going through a traumatic life- changing experience, I use my discretion to schedule duties and occasional paid time off. These are not secrets, since I inform other team members of my decisions and state that they're not to be seen as a precedent. There is a time when each member will have an extenuating circumstance that will need the leader's discretion.

I can only use my discretion when team members confide in me. While I don't need details, I need to know what they're dealing with to be able to apply discretion.

When Archibald's son was hospitalized, for several days he left the office early without informing anyone. When I spoke to him about his absenteeism, he explained that he had used all of his vacation time and could ill afford to take unpaid leave since he faced hefty bills. His unapproved absenteeism could have brought my leadership into question since I couldn't account for his whereabouts. His failure to communicate his circumstances left me exposed, and I couldn't cover for him. He understood that while I didn't need the details of his son's illness, he needed to inform me of the circumstances. I have a right to the information that impacts my ability to supervise and account for my team members.

I have the right to decide how to treat my staff. The organization's policies and procedures provide guidelines and are there to protect the leader, members, and organization. Within the parameters, I can determine how I treat team members. When I allowed team members to select the training programs they wanted to attend, I was deviating from the organizational policy that leaders select the relevant training program. However, my decision still falls within the organization's procedures.

I have a right to work with adults. I challenge team members to bring their adult selves to the office and work with me. I want to work with people who take responsibility and are not afraid to take risks.

I have a right to be treated as an adult. I don't shout at team members, or disrespect them; I don't call them names or insult them, and I expect to be treated the same way.

I have a right to make decisions for the team. As a leader, I have final veto power on everything the team proposes or decides. While this goes against the participatory nature of the team, I make no excuses when I have to stand alone and make a decision that is contrary to the team's opinion. This is ultimately my responsibility.

I have a right to determine how I want to lead. Members who do not appreciate my style are free to leave with no hard feelings. If a member is resisting my style, I offer transfer as an option and get involved in helping him find a team that's a better fit. Some team members unfortunately cannot move on and we end up stuck with one another. With these members, I continue to interact just as I do with all the others, and as long as they follow the rules of the space and deliver the work, it doesn't matter how they feel about the space.

As a leader, I don't have a right to loyalty. Members can say what they want about the safe space idea as well as about me. My ego knows better than to take these statements personally. This is a form of feedback that I need to sift through and glean for relevance. I take it as a learning opportunity to see what I may need to change or do differently. The hurt that I feel is tied to the fact that I think the safe space is a great idea, so I am likely to be peeved when someone disagrees. However, dislike for the space or for me doesn't take away the trust members have in me.

I have a right to honesty. I want people to speak the truth about what works and what doesn't work, and to tell me when I'm wrong.

I expect members to work each day they come to the office, and I expect them to do the things they are supposed to do within stated deadlines. I expect members to fail, to learn from their failures, and to start projects over again. I expect members to be afraid of taking risks but to take them anyway because the space supports them. I expect high-quality output from the team. This is the return on the time invested in members' development—the time spent planning, mitigating risks, transferring skills, building confidence, sorting out the lessons learned from failures, and supporting them to go again. This is the reason for the space.

CONCLUSION

I have a right to win. This is what I demand for the use of the space. I uphold my part of the bargain and hold the space for the members on the condition that I win. I actively keep the space safe for the team so we both can claim victory. I do all these things to achieve the vision I set for myself and the vision I set for the team. I have a right to work with a winning team, and the safe space provides the environment to make it happen.

Change Management

The team and I work with the safe space on a daily basis. We invoke the rules at team meetings, and when members pop into my office they double-check that they're in a safe space and proceed to unload, and then return to their duties. Sometimes they need to be coached and other times they don't. I play it by ear. They feel free to question, disagree, challenge, and—most importantly—to fail.

After two years of consistently applying the rules, dealing with the violations, taking risks, and winning, we have learned how to use the space and protect its integrity. Initially, however, each member resisted the idea in direct proportion to their levels of trust with me as the leader and their past experiences with innovative concepts. The members who trusted more resisted less, and those whose past experiences showed that efforts to adopt new things usually bombed tended to resist more. The team members also resisted the space in proportion to how much power they perceived they would be losing.

Matt was a charming sweet-talker who had previously used his wiles to get away with missing deadlines. He resisted the change since the even playing field destroyed his power base, and charm no longer equated to privileges. Stripping Matt of his power gave other team members confidence in the space.

Whatever is perceived as power by the team collectively or by the individual members will shift with the introduction of the space. There are no stars and no losers in the space; each member is equal and gets the authority and responsibility to gain personal achievements.

In addition to the reasons already mentioned, members resisted the space because of fear and associated feelings of powerlessness. They had to step out of their comfort zone and make an effort to change because they were being required to change.

FEAR

The space between what we want and where we are now is called anxiety. This sense of not knowing creates fear and our reaction is to resist. Members were unfamiliar with the idea and what it meant for them and therefore they were afraid. The safe space asked members to take risks and trust that the leader would stand with them in times of failure. Members were wary about whether the leader would provide a safety net, especially if this was contrary to their past experience.

COMFORT ZONE

In the past, the rules of engagement were clear. Delivering what the leader wanted meant survival in relative comfort, which brought members a sense of control. The safe space changed the rules of engagement since success was no longer prescriptive. Relationships with the leader had to be renegotiated and members had to learn new means of survival, and this increased the likelihood of mistakes. Team members could no longer share the responsibility for the failure; instead, members were expected to contribute to the winning formula. The space created a new working environment that led to the renegotiation of all boundaries as the status quo shifted. Members resisted the discomfort brought on by the new situation.

Being asked to bring their personal selves to work also added a new dimension, as members felt more vulnerable and exposed in the space.

EFFORT

Members made mental and emotional adjustments as they juggled new levels of freedom and authority with responsibility. They faced questions designed to provoke new thinking and understanding about what, why, and how events unfolded in the space. Members were asked to make more substantial contributions and be more involved in the required work. The role of each member's job was expanded and each person had more to think about and do.

Each member had to abide by the rules and sanction unsavory

behavior that the leader had previously handled alone. Some members resented the level of effort the safe space demanded from them.

PERSONAL BENEFIT

People embrace change when a personal choice is made for self-improvement or achievement. If members can't envision benefiting from assuming more responsibility or they see the space as beneficial only to the leader, they may resist the safe space. Members who embraced the space solely for the work benefits bailed when they realized the space included a personal growth journey—something they didn't want to embark on.

The leader is responsible for helping the team embrace the safe space. She needs to be patient as members come to terms with the changes and help as the team steadily adjusts through the initial fear and uncertainty of using the space.

MANAGING CHANGE

The leader can draw on the following recommendations from change management experts to help the team through the transition.

Essence

The leader needs to share the most essential or most vital part of the idea or experience. The central meaning or theme of the safe space needs to be discussed with the team. The safe space is designed specifically for the team to win. When the team identifies its vision and mission, the leader needs to determine how these fit in the organizational context and if they will allow the team to win. Everything the team does needs to be aligned to the vision and the goals. The roles the team adopts and the projects the team undertakes are part of getting the team to win. When team members concluded that the previous configuration limited opportunities for success, they decided to embrace the safe space.

Explanation

During and after establishing the space, I constantly communicated with the team members individually and as a group. My messages about the space and the reason for it were consistent. We discussed the rules, sanctions, and breaches. I brought organizational issues to the table to give the team the confidence to query and to challenge. I worked patiently with members who needed further explanations, treated them fairly, answered their questions, and gave them time to understand.

Engagement

Involving members in setting up the space gave them a sense of control, which helped reduce the feelings of anxiety as they made the space theirs. When things got difficult and they were uncomfortable, they stayed the course because they had set up the operating rules and were obligated to accept the outcome.

Enticements

Team members were complimented for all successes, and failures were used as talking points. I offered no tangible rewards other than those proposed by the company. I thanked members in written notes or emails that were copied to the entire team, and praised them in front of the peers. I do not believe in nor do I use negative incentives since they reinforce negative thinking around the space and the sinister reasons behind it.

While tangible rewards were received annually in the form of bonuses and promotions, members received intangible rewards when their peers recognized the changes in their authority and autonomy levels.

BENEFITS

The safe space needs to be seen as pivotal to the team's success in order for members to fully embrace the concept. As a result, all wins and benefits gained by members—team success, promotions, and changes in attitudes—were linked or attributed to the space and how it works. This positively reinforced that the safe space worked.

GRIEF

With change there is always a hankering for the good old days. The comfort zone is an alluring place; we know its ills and have found the ways to work around it that more or less get us what we need. We know how to tailor our desires so we're not disappointed, and giving up that comfort can be difficult.

Members will feel loss for the old ways of doing things as they encounter new challenges in the safe space. The extent of these feelings of loss will be determined by how radically different the safe space approach is compared to the way they previously operated. Leaders should expect and allow members to grieve the past.

When members spoke about "the way things were" or began sentences with "Our previous manager," I knew they were grieving for the comfort of the past. I put the expressions in the context of the Kübler-Ross grief model that states that persons experience five stages of grief when dealing with loss. The stages are not always experienced sequentially, nor does everyone experience each stage.

I have witnessed team members express grief over losing the status quo as they moved to accept the safe space. There was little I could do except wait for them to accept that the safe space was here to stay.

Denial

Team members often didn't believe they had the power or permission to take charge of their work. Some refused to take initiative and waited for instructions, operating in a fake reality until they realized that the way things had been done previously was no longer relevant to the current scenarios. Many members remained in denial and ignored the changes as they dealt with the pain of adjusting to the new way. As they wallowed through disbelief, all I could do was support them through it.

Anger

This showed up in every team member in different ways. Members resented that the game had changed and that they had to take on more responsibility to win. They were annoyed that they needed to plan and take charge of their careers and that they were required to perform at new standards. The resented the new type of questions, since all they wanted was an answer and a certain path forward. Those unaccustomed to honest feedback and those who resented an even playing field were also angry. The safe space was new territory, but they were charged with responsibility for it and they thought it unfair since it was my decision as leader that they had to change. The anger was often targeted toward me as they transferred their discomfort with the new situation. I accepted this as part of the course, kept my focus on the end result, and we got through it.

Bargaining

As the members tried to make sense of the loss, they tried to bargain about the quality of work, the application of the rules and sanctions, and the levels of authority they had. They put forward plausible reasons the space wouldn't work and the reasons the organization wouldn't support it. They argued, pleaded, and tried to withhold work as they bargained over the space. I reminded them why the space was established and remained consistent in the application of the rules of the space. I held up the department vision and mission to help them refocus on the loftier purpose so they could shift the focus from their pain to the agreements that were made.

Depression

When some members realized they had failed at negotiating changes, they seemed depressed, knowing they were powerless to influence the inevitable. They were doubtful that they could succeed in the new environment. These members said they were extremely worried about their ability to complete assignments. I tried to explain that the anxiety was only natural as we adjusted to using the safe space. This helped some of the members, but others had to wade through their feelings.

Acceptance

Eventually, team members accepted the change and acted accordingly. Even though this behavior is the last stage in the grief cycle, members still became angry or depressed and attempted to negotiate a different outcome. When the members realized I was constant in the approach and wasn't wavering from the decision, they ultimately all came around at different times and accepted the space.

THE LEADER'S ROLE

A leader needs to be patient and introduce the concept over a period of time. On occasion, I have made the mistake of giving team members too much responsibility since they seemed comfortable with the concept. After noticing the doubt and depression creep in, I had to scale back on the responsibilities and later increase them as members got more accustomed to the idea.

When I joined the new team and told the members about the idea, they were uncertain how it would work since it was in direct contrast to their previous work setting. They needed to get accustomed to the concept, and I needed to wait for that to happen.

Leaders need to anticipate that the team will have difficulty with the changes and be prepared for this. I had no incentives to offer, except the promise that the idea would lead to wins and that members could take charge of their work and develop new and exciting roles. I made the promise based on my assumptions that people always want to do better and have an improved experience. I said that I wanted to work with adults and therefore needed to give them room to be adults and full control over the way they worked; this was the only way I knew how to do this.

CONCLUSION

Change management is solely the leader's task. You've decided to adopt a new way of leading your team because it benefits you to work this way. While your team members are trying to understand how it works and its benefits for them, you need to manage their transition. As the change agent, the leader must increase his level of awareness and mindfulness of team members.

20

Culture

The organization is an unnatural organism constructed to serve a purpose; it operates with a set of assumptions that allow it to control and give a sense of order and predictability to its internal and external environments. This is expressed by the norms, values, beliefs, and habits that are supported in the environment and evidenced by the strategies, policies, and procedures governing the way people operate and make decisions within the organization. Over time this becomes the organizational culture that determines what is said and done, the way people dress and behave, and the things that are considered taboo.

Each team in the organization has its own subculture; each team leader espouses the key ideas for working successfully with him and so governs the way his team behaves and works. The safe space is the subculture for my team; it's the way I have determined that I want to work with a team. My role is to ensure I balance this subculture with that of the larger organization, paying particular attention to where it may be at odds with the organization's culture.

Team members seem pleased with the results of the space. They work confidently knowing that the safe space honors their creativity and intelligence and allows them to do more than a job description and more than they thought was possible. They want to spread use of the safe space to the other parts of the organization and champion the safe space to other teams. I hesitate and point out to them that's not our role.

Unless hired to do so, I don't think of myself as responsible for the organization's culture; and as a result, I don't promote the concept to other managers. I manage my team by those principles. I respect that other team leaders are managing teams as effectively as they know how. I stay out of their business and draw the line sharply around mine. When asked my opinion, I share my experience; but I do not tell others what to do. My hope is that other leaders will see the results of the idea and become intrigued enough to use the space with their own teams.

The safe space grows by osmosis. When I meet with other teams, I share the assumptions that everyone in the room is intelligent and creative enough to solve problems or achieve the set objectives. I encourage the development of rules and invite participants to use whatever they have found interesting in their own team meetings. Some people get it and begin to treat their teams in similar fashion. Team members also spread the safe space when they work collaboratively with others. When Jane worked with the sports club members, she led them to set up rules that encouraged frank and open discussions, which resulted in better events for the staff. Other team members promote safety when they collaborate with peers and glean from their experiences ways to develop work programs and to solve problems.

At times, I am sharply reminded that the organizational culture is bigger than the team's culture and that other parties may reject the fact that my team members are creative and intelligent. When Wendell was named project manager for the customer service project, other team leaders didn't believe he was competent enough to do the job and rejected his leadership. The project came to a screeching halt when they said I'd misjudged the importance of the project in the organizational context by putting him in charge. I coached Wendell through the rejection and visibly inserted myself as the project sponsor. As the team leaders began to trust his competence, I eased myself out of the limelight and left him to manage the project.

I don't feel pressured by what other leaders think. They don't have to agree with the methodology. I'm in charge of my team and determine how to treat the members, just as other team leaders decide how to treat their members.

Margaret, one of my team members, was challenged by Jack when she chaired a meeting of his peers. He refused to cooperate and loudly stated his displeasure with her approach. She didn't take his outburst personally; she used "what" and "how" questions to get the meeting back on track and led the participants to consensus on the issues at hand. When Margaret returned to the office, we analyzed the events. Her conclusion was that Jack questioned her authority to conduct a meeting with team leaders who were all her seniors.

When other teams or leaders question the amount of power members have, resist being led by my team members, suggest I'm not in control of the team, or express concern that this isn't the way they're accustomed to working, it suggests that the safe space is counter to the larger organizational culture. My role, then, is to protect the safe space from the external organizational influences—most of which I have no control over. I invite team members to discuss how the space differs from the prevailing organizational culture, and help them analyze the reactions and behaviors they experience. The emphasis is on understanding that even with the best of intentions, everyone will not agree that members should be empowered, and they will resist solely on that basis.

My job is to tell the wider organization that I have divested my authority in my team members. I take members to meetings as scribes or silent observers so people get accustomed to them being in the room. Over time I give members more responsibility in those rooms and eventually hand over the reins completely. This way, the wider organization gets familiar working with members in a leadership role and demonstrates that team members have my authority and trust to act in my stead. Team members are cautioned to be sensitive because their peers may not be working in the same manner as they are, and bragging is discouraged.

Organizational culture often results in shared mental assumptions about people. Most people bring only a part of themselves to work, so the organization falsely constructs a one-dimensional view of individuals and defines them by a label. This label predetermines the person's behaviors, and the organization shares a silent consensus about how that person should be treated. When Sharon was labeled a perfectionist, she thought this celebrated her high standard of work; however, it was translated as Sharon having a nit-picking attitude and people didn't want her to lead them.

Kerwin had a great sense of humor and was labeled the funny guy who made jokes—much to the delight of his peers. But he realized his opinions were not being considered and complained that he wanted to be taken seriously. When asked what was keeping him back, he admitted his jokes hindered his cause.

I often ask team members, "How do you want people to view you?" I invite them to be their own public relations machine and sell by their actions the way they want to be seen. Just as they create the projects and take charge of work, they can define the way the organization views and speaks about them. Labels are perceptions that become the reality as people see and experience the behaviors that affirm the perception.

The organization will treat us as it perceives us, and everything we do will be viewed through this lens. When we don't consciously determine how we want to be seen, we give the organization the freedom to determine who we are

When Kerwin agreed that he was a funny guy, he took every opportunity to make a joke. When he changed his self-perception, he controlled the way that others viewed him.

Each team member has the power to change the way the organization perceives him or her. We make our world and co-create the labels that are put upon us.

The safe space is often questioned by onlookers. Everything that's done is scrutinized, and remarks are made indirectly. I've seen team members squirm at the attention, become uncertain about their autonomy, or want to defend the space. I remind them they report to me and therefore don't need to explain themselves or the way they work to anyone. As the team leader, I have to deal with any challenges to the space; the member's role is to work with me to keep the space safe.

CONCLUSION

Shifts in culture do not happen overnight. Therefore, it is unreasonable to expect that because one team does something that works for it, other teams will willingly adopt the same methodology. There's no point in telling other teams what they should do. The team is reminded that our space is not something we're doing for the entire organization. We're using the space for ourselves so that we can excel and win at our jobs.

Final Thoughts

As stated before, I created the safe space because it allows me to achieve my personal vision of "enhancing the lives of the people with whom I come into contact" every single day.

I coach people through their personal and professional transformations so they can live the lives they want. Working in an office offers me the opportunity to create safety for a team of people and treat each person as if they were my client—and to help them achieve their ambitions.

I created the safe space so I can win and have a winning team. Winning—and helping other people win—makes me feel good and provides the impetus for me to go to work each morning. I know that it is possible to win without the team, but it makes winning much easier and more fun when other people are rooting for me and me for them.

I created the space to make my job easier. I don't have to think of everything, don't have to be a know-it-all, can share the responsibility for work, and can be wrong at times.

The safe space allows me to be me. I don't have to pretend, or to be someone else. I can be my perfectly flawed self. I'm more human in the room, explaining my concerns about decisions, discussing the fear underlying my procrastination, or giving an answer to someone. I created the safe space as a place where I can work with adults who want to come to work. They're adults who view work as part of, and not separate from, their lives, and they're encouraged to bring all their skills, creativity, and intelligence to the office.

I created the safe space to celebrate the fact that we are all human, frail, vulnerable, and, at times, we all need help. Most people think the workplace is not the place for showing emotions. But feelings are part of our life; people get depressed, angry, sad, and upset; and like it or not, these emotions cross over into our work lives, sometimes preventing us from performing. The safe space promotes quality work and recognizes that when negative emotions are running high, the team member cannot be productive. The space helps the member get rid of the emotion so he can get back to work.

The safe space was co-created with the team. The team established the rules and determined how the space would be used. The team is also responsible for maintaining the space and enforcing the rules around it. In the safe space, members are given freedom and learn to be responsible with the authority and autonomy they receive. Members are free to challenge the status quo and to determine what will take the organization forward, and given free rein to generate the projects that will allow this to happen.

In the space we focus on the work. We operate with a shared motive and assume that each team member makes decisions from this point of view. Winning is viewed from the team's viewpoint, and not that of one single member or the leader. In the space, members become self-directed, take charge of their daily work, and align these tasks to their overall career goals. Members focus on accomplishments, getting the wins they need to take the next step in their careers. The team celebrates wins and commiserates over losses. Each success and failure is scrutinized so we can learn to either replicate success or limit the recurrence of failure. Members take on risks in the space without fear of failure, as risks are considered stepping-stones in the winning process.

The space works because the team makes it work. Members will consciously or unconsciously violate the space, but the leader needs to intervene and get everyone back on track.

The leader has a critical role to play in maintaining the credibility of the space. She needs to be seen as honest and trustworthy for the team to fully trust the space. This calls on her to self-assess on a regular basis to ensure she's being consistent and fair in her treatment of team members.

People from other teams have used the space to explore ideas and concerns knowing that it's safe, that they're not judged, and that what they say remains confidential.

The safe space is not just for the office. The team members create safe spaces for each other at their cubicles so they can test ideas and get help with projects. Team members claim they've extended the concept with their spouses to have tough discussions and with their children so the kids are free to tell them anything and not be judged.

Setting up the space is not always easy. The space changes the way people behave and think. Members are asked to view work as an extension of their personal lives and to remove the walls between the two. They're encouraged to bring dimensions of themselves to the office, which many have never done before.

The safe space is not immediately going to work perfectly. There's a learning curve for the leader and the members. Openness and constant communication greatly help the team to get over the humps. Stick in there, check in regularly with the team and each member, smooth out problems when they happen, and put measures in place to deal with them.

Once the leader has tried the safe space and shared it with her team, she needs to let it go. The idea is no longer hers; it's now up to her team, and members will choose whether they will adopt it. Coercion contradicts the space.

Team members say that other teams notice our team gets things done with relative ease and that it seems a fun place to work. The members know the space and the way they work sets them apart from other teams. Team members approve of the space because they have reaped the rewards of having it.

One thing I know for certain is that people want to be led. My team members are creative, intelligent, and want to do better. I extend my knowledge to them, and they take what they need and apply it as they see fit. They don't need me to take care of them; they need me to show them how to navigate the organization and help them succeed. They want me to share with them what has worked for me and help them discover what works for them.

The space changes the outlook team members have of them-selves, of leadership, and of what is possible in the organization. Team members walk a little taller, speak with much more confi-dence, and rack up achievements.

*   *   *

I am proud that I've made a significant impact in the office and have influenced the way team members think. They mirror the safe space in the way they conduct meetings and interact with their peers. I am resolute in my commitment to continue experi-menting with the concept, improving and changing it as neces-sary. And I hope that you can join me in doing the same.

Photo courtesy of Shirley Bahadur

About the Author

Maxine Attong has been leading small and large teams for the last two decades both in organizational settings and in her private coaching and facilitation practice. She has helped organizations come to consensus, overcome the perils of ineffective leadership, redesign processes to suit changing environments, and manage the internal chaos inherent in strategy implementation.

She has been trained as a Gestalt Organizational Development practitioner, a Certified Evidence Coach, a Certified Professional Facilitator, a Certified Professional Accountant, and is a former Quality Manager.

Starting with her own vision of "enhancing the lives of the people with whom she comes in contact," Maxine collaborates with clients first to raise mindfulness and awareness of issues, and then to develop and implement strategies aligned to the organizational vision. This approach follows from her personal philosophy that all humans are intelligent, creative, and want to do better.

Her first book, *Change or Die: The Business Improvement Manual*, shares her "ENGAGE" Business Process Improvement methodology that empowers teams to effectively redesign processes within their companies, regardless of the industry within which they operate

In this second book, *Lead Your Team to Win: Achieve Optimal Performance by Providing a Safe Space for Employees*, which she considers her "heart" book, she details how she has created a "safe space" for team members to take risks and excel both within an organizational context and in their personal lives.

Maxine is a graduate of the University of the West Indies, and divides her time between the Caribbean and the US.

www.ingramcontent.com/pod-product-compliance
Lightning Source LLC
Chambersburg PA
CBHW021931220326
41598CB00061BA/1044